REVIEWS

"*This Is Getting Old* is wry and dry—funny and bracingly honest. Paul Taylor is amusing and upfront about himself, boomers, marriage, purpose, health problems, and home renovation. Beautifully written and a delight from start to finish."

—MARC FREEDMAN, author of *How to Live Forever: The Enduring Power of Connecting the Generations*

"With breezy wit and self-deprecating charm, Paul Taylor invites us into the intimate trials of aging, his careers as a journalist and social analyst, and his struggling optimism about his country. It is a memoir of pain and vision, gracefully written and deeply engaging."

—DAVID K. SHIPLER, Pulitzer Prize–winning author and former New York Times correspondent

"Paul Taylor's deeply informed and beautifully written memoir of two married boomers' personal and societal reckoning—poignant, amusing, thought-provoking, and ultimately hopeful—is a cross-generational pleasure. This is must reading for anyone who cares about who we are, how we got here, and what comes next."

—RICHARD NORTH PATTERSON, New York Times bestselling fiction author and political commentator

THIS IS GETTING OLD

*Two Boomers and
Their Generation at Dusk*

PAUL TAYLOR

ISBN: 979-8995223900

Produced by Publish Pros | PublishPros.com

Cover photo by Sarah Navarro
Back cover photo by Marianne Edmonds

AuthorPaulTaylor.com

CONTENTS

CHAPTER ONE

IT'S WEIRD THAT I'M THE SAME AGE AS OLD PEOPLE

I walk like an old man. Never used to. Stiff, slightly bent. Not yet a shuffle, no longer a stride. This isn't the worst thing ever to happen to anybody, but I gotta say, it sucks. My wife Stefanie says I look like a cowboy after a hard day's ride. As a kid I wanted to be a cowboy, so you'd think maybe that takes away some of the sting? Sorry, nope.

I'm not here to whine. When it comes to growing old, I have it easy. Others have it worse.

My beautiful wife is slowly going blind. She's had 27 eye surgeries over the past dozen years. She can't drive; she has a hard time recognizing faces; she gets startled by things that seem to sneak up on her; she's become a one-woman wrecking crew in the kitchen; she can no longer make jewelry or pottery or stained-glass. On top of that – and totally unrelated – she's developed a strange movement disorder that forced her to give up running.[1] Periodically she'll come home from her daily six-mile walk tilted wickedly to the left. Or sometimes to the right. She's been seen by a bunch of specialists, including a whole gang of them at the National Institutes for Health, which happens to be located just a few blocks away from our house in Bethesda, Maryland. She's stumped 'em all. Eventually they each get around to saying pretty much the same thing: You're such an interesting patient! You're such a healthy-looking sick person! And we have no frigging idea what's wrong with you! "And then," as Stefanie likes to put it, "they fire me."

So, yes, my wife has it a lot worse than I do. But of course, so many of our friends have it worse than either of us. We have friends with Parkinsons, friends with MS, friends with Alzheimer's, friends with heart problems, friends with stroke damage, friends with diabetes, friends with depression, friends with worn out body parts, friends whose careers cratered, friends whose marriages blew up, friends who've outlived their money, friends who've outlived their children, friends who've buried their spouses, and friends whose cancer treatments are as bad as their cancer symptoms, which are horrible. And we have a mounting tally of friends who aren't friends any more. They're dead.

You live long enough, apparently this is how it goes. And yes, we're not the first people this has happened to. Apparently it happens to just about everybody. But it's the first time it's happened to us!

First time, too, for our generation. Stefanie and I are Baby Boomers, the healthiest, wealthiest and most selfish generation ever to round third and barrel toward home. We got our name for being born and our fame for being young. We sorta figured we'd stay "forever young," as Bob Dylan put it. And while we were at it, save the world.

---

[1] *When she could run, she could run forever. If you toted up all the miles she covered in half a century of running, Stef circled the globe four-and-a-half times.*

Well, here we are now on the front stoop of old age – and good Lord what a fuck-up of a generation we've turned out to be. On our watch, America has suffered a collapse in economic mobility, social trust, civic faith, and family formation. A nation that used to be young and scrappy has gotten old and cranky. We're aggrieved, tribal, stuck. We can't find our can-do. We can't agree on what's real and what's fake. Our public life chokes on its own bile. Each political party thinks the other is not merely misguided but evil. They collaborate only to bury future generations in debt. Or to create four-hour airport waiting lines. Or to preside over a sometimes-violent culture war. Whenever blood is shed or someone gets killed, we repair to our corners and grieve in red and blue.[2]

By all means blame this hellscape on Donald Trump, the boomer-in-chief who's back in the White House with his blowtorch aimed at America's values, norms, laws, alliances and common decency. Blame it, too, on the 49.8% of voters who, with eyes wide open, sent him there.

But spare a few fingers to point at the entire boomer generation – the reds, the blues, everyone in between. We've been pretty much running the show in America for the past four decades. Boomer candidates have won eight of the last nine presidential elections – two Democrats (Clinton and Obama); two Republicans (Trump and Bush); all four elected twice. Boomer politicians occupy 60 of the 100 seats in the U.S. Senate. Boomer voters have been the largest age cohort in the electorate since the early 1980s.

No other American generation has ever wielded so much political power for so long. Nor has any generation ever done so much to

---

2   *A 2026 Pew survey found that 53% of Americans believe their fellow citizens have bad morals and ethics. Of 25 countries surveyed, the U.S. is the only one where a majority of the population holds itself in such low regard. In the U.K., 82% see their fellow citizens as morally good; in Mexico, 83%; in India, 88%; in Canada, 92%.*

enrich itself at the expense of the young. We were gifted the American Dream on a platter. We're passing along the table scraps.

And the young have noticed. Most doubt their standard of living will match that of their parents. (They're right). Fewer than a quarter say they trust the government, the media or their fellow human beings. A majority say they're embarrassed by our country. "When I make the case for American values and historic greatness, my son looks at me the way you look at a baby," laments boomer novelist Anne Lamott.

All this has played out in an era when America is undergoing unprecedented demographic, social, racial and technological change. We're enroute to becoming a majority non-white country at the same time a record high share of us is going gray and a record low share is making babies. These overlapping dramas have produced the widest chasm we've ever seen between the old (mostly white and conservative) and the young (mostly neither). A chasm over what, you ask? Oh, just the little stuff: identity, politics, religion, race, sex, gender, ethnicity, culture, marriage, patriotism, social media, news consumption. Assuming the death rate holds steady at 100%, the generational baton will eventually pass and our culture, politics and institutions will be transformed. For the better? Let's hope. But getting from here to there is going to be a shit show. Already is. Maybe you've noticed.

Back when I was a newspaper reporter, I wouldn't have packed so much oomph into those last few paragraphs. "Never write never," a grizzled editor told me when I was a cub. "You'll never be right." Later in my career I helped run a social science research institute. We called it a "fact tank." Most of my colleagues had PhDs. Like journalists, they were observers by temperament and training, with a boundless curiosity about human nature and a talent for asking good questions. Their looking glasses were different from those I'd learned to use in newsrooms. But they too had their admonitions. "If you're not God, bring data."

You want data? Here's some data: When Stefanie and I were coming of age amidst the craziness of the late 1960s, fewer than one in ten Americans told pollsters that they'd settle in another country if they had the chance. Today, one in three say they'd emigrate if they could. Huge change! But hold on a sec. Only about two percent of Americans today actually *do* live abroad. So that survey question measured a big change in attitudes, not behaviors. An important distinction. And a useful caveat. Surveys often illuminate, but in the wrong hands or context, they can deceive. Nobel Prize winning economist Ronald Coase put it well: "If you torture the data long enough, it will confess to anything."

At the Pew Research Center, where I used to work, we tried very hard not to torture our data. And we produced a ton of it! We asked questions about aging, about the generation gap, about our political tribes and our culture wars, about changing racial attitudes, gender identities, household arrangements and marital trends, about social and religious values, about immigration patterns, about news consumption habits and social media behaviors, about economic well-being, about labor force participation, about human happiness – about anything and everything we could measure with public opinion surveys, Census findings, election returns and news content analyses. At around the time Trump came down his golden escalator, I crammed a bunch of that data into a book, *The Next America,* which tried to shed some light – and throw some shade – on the whole godawful mess.

You can divide my working life in half. For the first 25 years, I was a newspaper reporter. For the second 25, a political and media reformer, a demographer, a pollster, an author and a public speaker. The through-line is a conviction that democracies can't survive unless they're built on a foundation of facts. In an age when trolls, deepfakes, shit-posters and conspiracy peddlers seem to have the whip hand, the work done by empiricists like me has never been as important. Or as challenging. Or as unheeded. But one thing hasn't changed. It's still a blast.

This book is two for the price of one. I'll take a whack at chronicling how our politics and public square became so toxic. And I'll try to explain how a generation that came of age crusading for individual liberties and social justice is stuck at dusk arguing about pronouns, vaccines and halftime shows.

But the bigger part of the book is a much smaller story. It's a coming-of-old-age memoir about Stefanie and me and our lifelong love affair. It's about the magical summer community in the Adirondacks where we met as toddlers and where we now watch our grandkids swim in the same lake and build castles in the same sand we played in as little kids. And frolic with playmates whose grandparents played with us when we were young. Grandparents who are taking the same bumpy ride into old age that we are.

It's also about an audacious project that Stefanie and I embarked on shortly after we both turned 71 – expanding the vacation home here in paradise we inherited from Stefanie's folks. Two boomers raging against the dying of the light.

We've pulled this off mostly with our own hands. We've been at it for five years. It's finally done! (OK, almost). It's been unfathomably rewarding and hugely challenging. We gutted and rebuilt the kitchen, added a new dining room, deck and portico, and somehow built 50 feet of winding stairs down a steep slope to the creek below. We clad all twenty-two exterior walls in gorgeous cedar trucked down from a sawmill north of Lake Placid. We rebuilt most of the floors, some of the ceilings and all the bathrooms, put up a new roof, put in a new laundry room, replaced or reframed 41 windows, repainted most of the rooms (the living room four times until we got the color right) and built a lovely little waterfall alongside the new stairs to our new front entrance. For the most demanding jobs we got lots of help from our son-in-law, a couple of local handymen and assorted plumbers and electricians, all of whom are way more skilled than we are. Could never have pulled this off without them. But day in and day out, year in and year out, it's been mostly us. Me with the table saws, chop saws, circular saws, rotating saws, screw guns, hammers, drills, wrenches, levels, squares, miter boxes, drywall knives, chisels, pry bars, joist hangers, caulk, joint compound, putty, corner bead, flashing, picks, shovels, mauls, mallets, shingles, post-hole diggers, cinderblock, plywood, pine studs, cedar boards, hemlock rafters, 1x3s, 1x4s, 2x4s, 2x6s, 2x8s, 2x10s, 2x12s, 4x4s, 4x6s, 4x8s, 6x6s, 6x8s, 8x8s, Tyvek, Trex, Sheetrock, Sacrete and Great Stuff; me dangling from ladders, scaling slopes, hauling lumber, stacking rocks. Stefanie as the general contractor, the kitchen designer and – low vision be damned – the wall and floor tiler. Stefanie as the worrier-in-chief, though I put in my time there too. Both of us on endless shopping trips together to Home Depot, Lowes, Ace Hardware, Tractor Supply, Harbor Freight, Lumber Liquidators, Hill Electric, Curtis Lumber, Luzerne Hardware, the Tile Store, and an assortment of sawmills, stone quarries and plumbing supply houses. And us shopping together on the internet, where things often went poorly.

The project has been our shot at leaving a legacy. We threw everything we had at it – heart, mind, body, soul. And by God it's turned out better than our wildest dreams. Damn near perfect. But at a cost. For one thing, my knees sorta died on the job. And for another, Stefanie and I spent most of the time driving each other nuts.

When you've been married as long as we have, you'll get asked: "What's the secret?" Neither of us has ever come up with a good answer. Stef's stock response smacks of vaudeville: "Lack of imagination." What I can report, after 55 years, is that marriages never stop evolving. Ours hasn't. And not always for the better. Given all that's gone right for us – loving family, great friends, mostly good health – we should be gliding into our golden years on a magic carpet of harmony, happiness and gratitude. Yes, there's that. But there's also this: We've hurt each other's feelings more in the last five years than we did in the first fifty. Neither of us has adapted well to loss and decline. Stefanie has grown anxious; I've become bull-headed.

We're hardly the first old married folks who've had to cope with these plot twists and personality changes. They come with territory. "Wholly unprepared, [people] embark upon the second half of life… with the false presupposition that our truths and ideas will serve us hitherto," the Swiss psychiatrist Carl Jung wrote. "But we cannot live in the afternoon of life according to the programme of life's morning—for what was great in the morning will be little at evening, and what in the morning was true will at evening have become a lie."

As dusk descends, Stefanie and I are scrambling to rejigger the roles inside our relationship. So far we've done a lousy job. What used to come naturally now takes work. We need to adapt. All of this made the building of our masterpiece a pain in the ass as well as a triumph. It's led us to realize how different we are from each other. Maybe we always were? Hmm, not sure. Trying to figure this out. Next big project?

That's not all I'm trying to work out. For me, the worst thing about getting old has been facing up to how clueless I've been about so much stuff I thought I understood. For half a century I made a good living as a skilled observer of political and human behavior. Yet I never saw Trump coming. Never got my mind around the mess my generation has made. Never thought the shadow of authoritarianism would be at our doorstep. Never imagined the cruelty and crazy of the dark web. Never contemplated a post-fact world. Saw lots of the trees; somehow missed the forest. So here I am at twilight – a cockeyed optimist and raging empiricist heartsick for America, embarrassed for himself.

No tears, please. I'm an old white guy with an Ivy League degree who's had the deck stacked in his favor in more ways than he can count. Stale, pale, male, Yale. I grew up middle-class, attended good public schools and was raised in a home overflowing with unconditional love. When I was a little boy my mom told me the world was going to be my friend. Boy was she right! But when you get to be my age, a happy childhood and a lifetime of good fortune can't rescue you from being my age. Nobody gets a hall pass from getting old.

There's a scene in *War and Peace*, my dad's favorite novel, in which Count Nikolai Rostov has his horse shot out from under him during the heat of battle. As he runs for cover, he thinks to himself: "There must be some mistake. They're firing at me. Me, who everybody loves!"

That's how I feel about old age. *There must be some mistake. It's coming for me. Me, who everybody loves!*

I'm going to spend the rest of this memoir trying to get better at getting old. Trying to understand my country better. Trying to figure out how to save it. Trying to get my own mojo back. Before, um, you know.

If you're thinking about coming along for the ride, I've got a caveat and a promise.

The caveat: Don't pick up this book expecting to find the magic formula for staying forever young. I ain't got one. You're better off cruising TikTok, where a bustling industry of anti-aging influencers serves up a bottomless banquet of science and quackery. They treat aging as a curable condition, death an avoidable fate. Who knows, maybe one day someone will finally crack the case. But then what?

The promise: I'll try to keep the whining about the way I walk to a minimum. It would be better if I could shut up about it altogether, but no, I don't see that happening.

CHAPTER TWO

THE MESS WE MADE

*"They were careless people, Tom and Daisy – they smashed up things...
and let other people clean up the mess they had made." The Great Gatsy,
by F. Scott Fitzgerald.*

Stefanie and I belong to the generation that America loves to hate.
With our long reign about to come to an end, shall we take stock?

Might as well. Younger generations have already weighed in, not
with affection. A few years ago, "OK Boomer" ricocheted around
TikTok something like four billion times, as youngsters took turns
skewering us for greed, arrogance, entitlement, luddism and assorted lesser sins. Some boomers tried clapping back (participation tro-
phies, safe spaces, snowflakes), but our memes never lit up the internet. For my generation, online trolling is an away game.

Plenty of anti-boomer flak has also come from inside the tent. In
2014, humorist P.J. O'Rourke published *The Baby Boom: How It Got
That Way. And It Wasn't My Fault. And I'll Never Do It Again.* He called
us a collection of "willful, rash, careless, vain, indulgent, entitled

spoiled brats...who rule the world." But he managed to lob his broadsides playfully, even tenderly.

Boomer bashing took on a nastier tone after Trump first became president in 2017. Washington Post columnist Dana Milbank called him "a bright orange symbol of what went wrong with this massive generation...narcissistic, impulsive and uncompromising." Trump biographer Michael D'Antonio called him the "Me Generation boomer-in-chief."

It would take a couch full of psychiatrists to decipher whether someone with a personality as damaged as Trump's can symbolize anything beyond his own needy, cruel, soulless self. But Trump or no Trump, I fear the gist of the boomer indictment is spot on. We've brought America to a dark place.

Generalizations about generations require asterisks. Here are mine: We're not all bad people! Nor are we all alike. Politically, we're all over the map – liberal, conservative, independent. Indeed, if you think about all the ways America has changed over the past half century, you could summarize the boomer contribution in two sentences. We drove the change. And we drove the backlash.

But there's one trait that most boomers of all stripes share: a thirst for cultural combat, fueled by elevated levels of self-regard, self-interest and self-righteousness. When we were young, we waged a culture war against the old. Now that we're old, we're waging an economic war on the young. And all the way through, we've been at war with each other. No matter what our partisan or ideological leanings, we boomers have been certain of one thing above all. We know best.

Our swagger is a product of our upbringing. We were raised by parents who celebrated the end of World War II by having lots of babies and treating us like little princes and princesses. "Nothing was too good for a generation lucky enough to be spared the scars of the Depression and the war," *People* magazine editor Lanny Jones wrote in the 1980 book that gave us our name (*Great Expectations: America and the Baby Boom Generation*). "[Postwar] affluence would now bring their children the best of everything. They would have more toys, more money, and more attention. They would have better schools and better books and better teachers."

This has worked out extremely well — for us. Boomers have become the wealthiest generation in American history by far. Today we own $85 trillion in assets – more than half the nation's total wealth, even though we comprise just a fifth of its population.[3] Never before has a single generation held so big a slice of the American pie.

How did we pull this off? Hard work and grit, to be sure. Most of all, though, good timing. New York University's Edward Wolff, America's leading expert on generational wealth, attributes the "astonishing" growth of boomers' lifetime assets to a combination of fortunate economic conditions that prevailed throughout most of our working years. An expansion of middle-class jobs. Low housing costs. A long stock market boom, Favorable interest rates. Strong labor unions. Good pension benefits. No successor generation has felt so many tail winds. Today the average age of a first-time home buyer is 40. When we started out, it was 29. Today, roughly half of young adults are downwardly mobile. Only a small share of boomers are wealthy, but the vast majority of us have enjoyed a standard of living better than our parents'.

Along the way, we've transformed America's attitudes about wealth. We grew up in an era when egalitarian norms were the coin of the realm. The beloved entertainment cathedral of our youth – Disneyland – opened in 1955 as the "happiest place on earth" where "everyone is a VIP." Its theme song evoked the essence of American Dream: "When you wish upon a star, it makes no difference who you

---

[3]   *The figure is drawn from Federal Reserve data released at the end of 2025. Boomers today enjoy a median household wealth that, in inflation-adjusted dollars, is more than double what their parents' generation had at the same stage of life. They hold four times more wealth than the total population of Japan and five times more than the total population of Germany. The only foreign nation with more total wealth than America's boomers (barely – $91 trillion) is China, whose population is twenty times larger.*

are." But nowadays at Disney's theme parks, if one of your wishes is not to be stuck in long lines, it makes a big difference who you are. If you've got enough money, you can buy yourself VIP status and jump your family to the front of the queue.

A small tell about a huge shift. In Donald Trump's America, we're led by a government of, by and for billionaires – the culmination of a decades-long evolution in our values, norms and policies. Today the typical Fortune 500 CEO earns 300 times more than the typical worker; back in our youth, the ratio was twenty-to-one. Nowadays our news media updates multi-billionaire top ten lists as if they're the latest baseball batting averages. Last year the board of directors of Tesla put together a trillion dollar (!) compensation package to keep Elon Musk in the saddle as CEO. And in this New Gilded Age, the wealthy can pass their fortunes on to their children without Uncle Sam grabbing so much as a dime. Inherited wealth has always had an awkward place in our bootstrap-loving culture – envied, coveted, disdained. But now in our tax code, it's become a sacred cow. Nepo babies have us to thank for that.

Boomers have a Jekyll-and-Hyde relationship with future generations. When it comes to our own kids and grandkids, no generation of oldsters has ever been as generous.[4] With so much of America's wealth parked in our bank accounts and retirement funds, we can afford our munificence — and our kids need our money! The anthropologist Margaret Mead said families are "the only faithful human institution." As parents and grandparents, we've gilded this faithfulness with gobs of money and kept it flowing deep into old age – then beyond the grave, through inheritances.

But as citizens and taxpayers, we've closed our hearts and wallets to other people's kids. Along with burying them in debt, we've scaled

---

[4] *Six-in-ten of today's grandparents (most of whom are boomers) provide ongoing financial assistance to their offspring. Four in ten help care for their grandchildren on a regular basis. Ten percent of all grandkids reside with a grandparent.*

back on public investments in schools, research, infrastructure, and a wide range of future-friendly policies. The best explanation for this dichotomy is hiding in plain sight. For the first time in our history, most of today's kids are nonwhite. Many are the offspring of the giant post-1965 wave of immigrants that has turned the American tapestry into a coat of many colors. When most boomers drive by schoolyards and playgrounds, they don't see a future that looks like them.

The story boomers like telling about America is that here, you can start at the bottom and rise as high as your smarts, talents, and drive will take you. The American story that the young need to tell themselves is to choose your parents and grandparents wisely. The better off they are, the better off you're likely to be. Not a happy story, but a more accurate one. The richest 1 percent of U.S. families now own 32% of the nation's household wealth; the top ten percent own 67% and the bottom half owns just 2.5%. At the same time, our rates of intergenerational mobility have fallen behind those in other wealthy countries. Economically, we're more unequal than ever, and we're thrusting our inequality forward onto future generations.

～

Boomers are often cited as proof of the famous Churchill quip: "If you're not a liberal at age 20 you have no heart. If you're not a conservative at age 40, you have no brain."

Well, yes and no. Yes, as we made our way into middle age we migrated from hippie to yuppie, from altruism to narcissism, from social justice to creature comforts. Greed-is-good became a cultural mantra and boomers became a conservative juggernaut. But no, we were never the one-note band of wild-eyed radicals portrayed in those yellowed press clips from the Sixties. Back then, the war protesters and flower children grabbed all the headlines. But for every long-haired hippie at a campus sit-in, there was a buzz-cut high school grad wading through the rice paddies in Vietnam. That intra-generational divide tracked along lines of social class, education, race and ideology. Half a century later, those same fault lines still divide boomer nation.

I graduated from Yale in 1970, at the height of the Vietnam War. The United States still had a compulsory military draft. Nearly three million young Americans served in Vietnam during the decade of that war. I was not among them. By the grace of a lottery number of 317, I never had to face that draft. Astonishingly, none of my friends from college – or, for that matter, from my upper middle class public high school in Washington DC, or from my summer community in Lake Luzerne, N.Y – served in Vietnam either. This was beyond dumb luck. People like me opposed the war and knew how to work the system. For one of my college roommates, that meant inducing an asthma attack the morning of his draft physical. For chickenhawk Donald Trump, it meant conjuring up a killer case of bone spurs. Early examples of an enduring boomer trademark: Privilege protects itself.

From the get-go, the boomers' voting record skewed more conservative than generally understood. Pop quiz: In the 14 presidential elections of the boomer era, from Nixon's victory in 1972 to Trump's in 2024, how many times did a majority of boomers vote for the Democrat? Surprise answer: Just once (Carter in 1976). Yes, our generation has gotten more conservative as we've aged. But no, we were never all that liberal.

If one turns one's gaze from presidential elections to public policy, the conservatism of the boomer era becomes even more striking. My generation provided the big electoral muscles behind the Reagan Revolution, which reduced the role of government, cut taxes, slowed down the civil rights and environmental movements, protected corporate interests, gutted labor unions and promoted policies that helped the rich get richer.

I won't belabor these points; this isn't a partisan manifesto. But I will spend a moment unpacking the one overarching feature of boomer era public policy I find the most damning. My generation hasn't paid its way. We've taken care of ourselves and left the tab for younger generations. On our watch, America has done a most un-American thing: We've waged war on the future.

It's easy to make this case with a few numbers. In the 1970s, as boomers started to enter the workforce and pay taxes, the total national debt that the U.S. had accumulated over the previous two centuries stood below $1 trillion. Now it stands at $39 trillion and is on track to rise by another $20 trillion by mid-century. We're not the only voters responsible for this drunken sailor spending. But we're the biggest culprits. And it's not just the amount of debt we've piled up. It's how we've spent the money. Mostly on ourselves.

When boomers were young, the federal government spent $3 on programs that invested in the future for every $1 it spent on programs targeted for older adults. On our watch, that ratio has completely flipped. It now approaches $5 on older adults to $1 for children.

Most of this domestic spending now goes to support Social Security, Medicare and Medicaid. These programs are the crown jewels of the American social policy. They have radically improved old age. Because of them, fewer than one in ten older adults today is poor. Without them, nearly half would be poor.

Precisely because these programs are so vital, every generation has a responsibility to make sure they work not just for today's older adults, but for tomorrow's. This is a simple matter of generational equity. It is a test boomers and their elected leaders from both parties have abjectly failed.

Everyone who pays attention to these programs has known for decades that they are on a path to insolvency. The bean counters project that in six or seven years from now– by which time tens of millions of boomers will have collected full benefits and gone on to their greater rewards – the system will be able to pay out only about 75 cents for every dollar of promised benefits. Yet no elected leader of either party has lifted a finger to address the problem. They dare not risk the electoral wrath of the boomers. Instead, what we get from both sides of the aisle are passionate speeches about the need for reform, followed by partisan blue or red proposals that everyone knows have no chance in hell of becoming law. There hasn't been any comprehensive reform to Social Security since 1983, when a pair of ideological warriors from the Greatest Generation – Ronald Reagan and Tip O'Neill – laid down their arms long enough to push through a compromise package for the good of the country they both loved.

That helped to fix the problem for a while, but the math keeps mathing. The longer we wait to make another big fix, the deeper the fiscal hole and the more the burden of any solution will land on the young.

This is beyond negligence. It is generational theft. Today in America, children and young adults are the poorest generation. As they enter the workforce, they'll pay regressive taxes to support Social Security benefits for today's old at a level they themselves have no chance of receiving when they become old.

Here's what Nicholas Kristof, the indefatigable op-ed advocate for children, had to say about all this in a New York Times column on February 7, 2024:

"Individually, we adore and pamper our children. We shuttle them from soccer practice to music lessons and then organize their play dates with meticulous fanaticism.

"Yet collectively, we mistreat America's children, especially by the standards of other wealthy countries. When we're formulating policies for children as a whole rather than coddling our own little angels, we fall scandalously short. We prize children in the abstract but as a society tend to ignore their needs. Children are more likely to go hungry or live in poverty in America than in most of our peer countries, and they are also much more likely to die — because of drugs, guns, accidents and an inequitable health care system…"

Now that I've gotten good and worked up, I'll linger a moment longer to rant about two more boomer policy fiascos – climate and guns. No need to belabor either one. The facts are widely known.

I will, however, draw a distinction between the two. The failure to address the climate crisis is not a uniquely American phenomenon. The whole world has been slow. If ever there's been an issue in which the young have a greater stake than the old, this one is it. We've done better than some countries, worse than others. And belatedly, we've gotten more engaged – though in Trump's America, the impetus for change will have to come from the private sector, civic groups, local governments, and grass-roots activism.

Guns violence is a different matter. It is a uniquely American sickness. And it's gotten much worse on the boomers' watch. Quickly, a few numbers. We're the only country in the world with more guns than people. Gun-related homicides occur in the U.S. at 18 times the rate per-capita that they do in the rest of the world's developed countries. Gun-related suicides happen here at 10 times the rate of the rest of the world. As for mass shootings – the diabolical modern-era addition to our vile history of gun violence – they now happen in America at the astonishing rate of nearly two every single day. More than 70 percent of all mass shootings in the world happen in the U.S. We account for 4 percent of the world's population.

Every mass shooting is a horror, but the most grotesque are the ones that target children. In the past quarter century, 394,000 American children have experienced shootings in their schools.[5] Everyone remembers the worst of these slaughters. Columbine. Sandy Hook. Parkland. Uvalde. Children today can recite that list the way children in my day could talk about Valley Forge, Gettysburg, Iwo Jima and Omaha Beach. When I was a kid in school we did air raid drills, preparing for the nuclear attack that never came. Kids today

---

[5]   *That figure is from the Washinton Post, which, unlike the federal government, maintains a data base of school shootings. As of April 2025, there had been 428 school shootings since the Columbine massacre in 1999, leaving 216 dead and 487 injured. The pace has accelerated in recent years, topping 40 a year in both 2021 and 2022. Most school shooters are themselves children; their media age is 16. Yet somehow, some way, they've gotten their hands on a weapon of war.*

do active shooter drills, preparing for school slaughters that happen with grim regularity. We worried about bombs launched by distant enemies. They worry about that moody kid in fourth period science class. I wish I had something novel to say about how America fell into this dark place, and what we need to do to crawl out. I don't. It's all been said, over and over. We know the problems. We know the solutions. We just can't get there. Shame on us.

All of the above comprises a big part of what our grade school teachers used to call "our permanent record." There's no erasing it, no undoing it. But the boomers' legacy has other dimensions as well. When I began writing this chapter I got in touch with Lanny Jones, a long-time acquaintance, to solicit his thoughts about the boomers' final report card. Lanny, who passed away in 2024 at the age of 81, spent his career as the founding editor of *People* Magazine and the author of a handful of books on an eclectic range of topics. He initially begged off, saying he hasn't paid close attention to the boomers in the four decades since he coined the term.

Instead, we began by talking about the very notion of generations. Is there really such a thing, or are they mere confections, whipped together by hyperactive pulse-takers like the two of us? We both acknowledged some conceptual soft spots. Obviously, there are as many different personality types within any generation as there are across generations. (Look no further than the four boomers who've lived in the White House: Bill Clinton, George W. Bush, Barack Obama, Donald Trump). Then there's what I think of as the arbitrary boundary problem. It defies common sense that people who happen to be separated by just one birth year are automatically pooled into different generations. But that's what folks like me must do in order to create age-bound cohorts that we then slice and dice into data sets on our way to defining them as different generations and assigning them clever names.

Lanny said he's comfortable with his coinage because he based it on historic changes in the birth rate. On the subject of generations, he called himself a "demographic hardliner." When I asked what he thinks about other generations based on softer criteria, he said, "Mark me down as a skeptic."

I take a more generous view. Yes, generations are confections, but they're useful confections. They help explain ourselves to ourselves. And they pass a smell test. Given the breakneck pace of social, cultural, technological and demographic change, it stands to reason that people who come of age now have values, traits and world views different from those of us who came of age decades ago. No, not everyone in a generation is alike. Neither are all New Yorkers or all Texans. Neither are the Brits or the French. But there *is* a type. "Like all group differences, generational differences are based on averages," writes Jean Twenge, author of *Generations*. "Groups differ within themselves as well as between each other, but the group differences still exist."

When I coaxed my conversation with Lanny back to the boomers, he told me about the inspiration for his book. It made Twenge's point.

"I'm not a boomer myself. I was a child of the 1950s and had a very traditional upbringing. But I had one brother who was six years younger and another brother who was 12 years younger. Their life experiences as teenagers were radically different from mine – sex, drugs, rock and roll, the whole thing. I didn't need a sociologist to tell me how everything had changed. I could see it at the dining room table every night."

To answer to my questions about the boomers' legacy, Lanny emailed me an interview he did in 2021 with the person he had identified in his book as the first boomer – Kathy Casey Kirschling, who was born in Philadelphia a few seconds after midnight on Jan. 1,

1946. He had asked her how she saw the world – and her generation – as she turned 75.

"I wanted to put a human face on her generation, and, if nothing else, she would become my ur-boomer," Lanny wrote. "Growing up in a middle-class suburb, Kathy went through A-bomb drills at school, watched *The Mickey Mouse Club* on TV, and danced to Dick Clark's *American Bandstand*. She went to work as an X-ray technician and married a medical intern who went to Vietnam. Then she went to night school, had two daughters, and acquired two boomer badges, a BMW and a divorce.

"Now remarried and a grandmother of five, she and her second husband divide their time between Florida and New Jersey. She walks 30 miles a week and has made volunteerism a center of her life. She has traveled to help victims of Hurricane Katrina and impoverished families in Camden, New Jersey."

Kathy told Lanny that "the women's lib movement helped me feel all along that I was equal to any man. We have a place in all areas of teaching, medicine, space exploration, CEO of corporations and Supreme Court justice to vice president of the U.S. That has changed the nation and opened endless possibilities for our daughters and granddaughters. We have a seat at the table. We can make a difference and have made a difference."

"Does she have any regrets? 'We boomers did a lot of good but created a lot of problems. I have so many concerns about greed – how much money any one of us needs. Greed seems to dominate.'"

I think Lanny's ur-boomer has it exactly right. She put her finger on what's best and worst about the boomer legacy. I've said my piece about the bad stuff. Let's spend a little time on the good.

Boomers bounded onto the scene in the 1960s as champions of social justice and individual freedom. Most of the leaders of the great civil rights movements of that era came from the generation older than boomers, the so-called Silents. But as Twenge writes, "The Boomers' role in these movements was ultimately even more impactful: They made the core values of the counterculture mainstream. Silents changed laws and rules, but Boomers changed hearts and minds, toward not just equality but its real-world outcomes, from the entry of more black students into universities to the societal approval of women as professionals and leaders...."

I'm with Kathy: of all the liberation movements of the boomer era, the empowerment of women has been the most transformative. When I went to college, 60 percent of all BA's went to men. Today nearly 60 percent go to women. There's gender parity in graduate schools for medicine, law and business. In the workplace, the pay gap hasn't disappeared but has narrowed. In executive suites and legislative chambers, women are no longer curiosities. On the home front, the traditional male breadwinner/female homemaker template for marriage is now just one of many arrangements. In 45% of all heterosexual marriages today, the wife earns as much or more than the husband. Fifty years ago, that figure was 15%.

Progress never flows in a straight line. In 2023 the Supreme Court reversed Roe v Wade, depriving women of the reproductive rights they'd been guaranteed a half century earlier by a previous Supreme Court. The Me Too Movement has been an ugly reminder that predatory sexual behavior by some men is immune to changes in the culture.

Meantime, as the labor force participation rate of women has reached record highs, it has plummeted for men, especially young men, who struggle to find a life script in a society where being a provider is no longer an exclusively male preserve.

The diverging economic trajectories of young men and women have taken a toll on romance, sex,[6] marriage, fertility and the nuclear family, all of which are in a steep decline. In 1970, two-thirds of all 25-to-49-year-olds lived with a spouse and at least one child. Now just one-third do. When today's parents are asked about their hopes and dreams for their kids, 88% (according to a Pew survey) say it's extremely or very important for them to have a good job and become financially independent. By contrast, just 21% say the same about their children getting married or having children of their own. "Devoted parents [prod] their kids to prepare for the Big Career," says sociologist Kay Hymowitz. "When it [comes] to that other crucial life goal — finding a loyal, loving spouse, a devoted parent for their grandchildren — their lips [are] sealed."

This is not an America-only phenomenon; similar trends have taken hold throughout Europe and Asia. For most of human history, the two-parent nuclear family had been the primary institution for propagating the species and raising the young. In the blink of an eye, it has lost massive market share.[7]

Likewise, the falloff in human fertility is without precedent in human history. So too the rise in human longevity. Put the two together and you produce what demographers call an inverted age pyramid. Consider China. In 1950, there were 75 Chinese children under the age of 15 for every 10 Chinese adults over the age of 65. By

---

[6]   *"Are Young People Having Enough Sex?" asked the cheeky headline of a New Yorker book review in 2025. Apparently not. In 2023 The Atlantic ran a cover story on "The Sex Recession" and The Washington Post fretted over "The Great America Sex Drought." Their stories cited survey data showing that the rate of celibacy among young adults has doubled in recent decades. The leading culprits? Online porn and unmoored guys.*

[7]   *In the United States, the divergent life priorities of young men and women are widest when viewed through a partisan lens. A 2025 NBC survey of 18-to-29-year olds found that young men who had voted for Trump rated being married and -having children as their highest life priority, while young women who had voted for Harris rated it as the lowest priority among a dozen items tested.*

2050 there will be just 5 Chinese children under age 15 for every 10 Chinese adults over age 65. The fertility rate in China is now just 1.2 per woman. In neighboring South Korea, it has fallen even lower, to 0.7.[8] Those countries are extreme cases, but this is a global phenomenon. If current trends continue (and there's no guarantee they will), three quarters of all countries in the world will have birthrates below replacement level (2.1) by the middle of this century. The whole of Europe is already there. In 2025, a single African country, Nigeria, produced more babies than did all 44 European countries, including Russia.

As populations keep getting grayer, strains on social safety net programs will keep getting worse. A child born today in an economically advanced country has a 50/50 chance of living to be 95. What this means for the future of humanity is a question above my pay grade. Will small cohorts of workers be able to support large cohorts of retirees? Or will we be okay with fewer workers, because AI will be doing all the work anyway? I don't know. But I can confidently report this: We're conducting that experiment right now.

Speculation about the future of AI is such a compelling topic that I can't resist inserting a time capsule here that my grandchildren might read one day with – what? – amusement, horror, nostalgia, disbelief? Who knows? As I write in the spring of 2025, a big report has just emerged from Silicon Valley on the future of AI. It predicts that by the end of 2027, "AIs will be…fully autonomous agents that are better than humans at everything." Oh and by the way, the report's lead author, Daniel Kokotajlo, forecasts "with 70 percent certainty" that AI will eventually destroy or catastrophically harm humanity.

Most other AI futurists strike a happier note. But for reasons I can't fully explain, on this topic I'm with the Cassandras – which is

---

[8]   *In the U.S., lifetime fertility has fallen to a record low of 1.6 per woman. One reason it hasn't fallen even more is that immigrant women have more children than do the native-born.*

where most of the public is as well. My good friend and former Pew colleague Lee Rainie works with Elon University on a project called Imagining the Digital Future. He too just came out with a big report, this one based on surveys and interviews with hundreds of AI experts. Overall the forecasts were mixed, but Lee led the report with this sobering prediction about the impact of AI on human relationships from Nell Watson, president of EURAIO, the European Responsible Artificial Intelligence Office:

"By 2035…AI companions will offer relationships perfectly calibrated to individual psychological needs, potentially overshadowing authentic human connections that require compromise and effort. AI-driven entertainment, virtual worlds and personalized content will provide peak experiences that make unaugmented reality feel dull by comparison. Virtual pets and AI human offspring may offer the emotional rewards of caregiving without the challenges of the real versions. AI romantic partners could provide idealized relationships that make human partnerships seem unnecessarily difficult… Without careful development and regulation, these artificial experiences could override natural human drives and relationships, fundamentally altering what it means to be human."

Yikes!

Back to the boomers. Our record of expanding opportunities to racial minorities and LGBTQ Americans has been both breathtaking and incomplete. It also helped trigger the backlash that has made our politics so toxic. Boomers changed lots of hearts and minds; we didn't get 'em all. The same goes for the other profound transformation that had its origins in the 1960s – the opening of our borders in 1965 to the largest immigration wave in human history.

Unlike the 32 million immigrants of the 19th and early 20th centuries, almost all of whom were white Europeans, about nine in ten of the nearly 70 million boomer-era immigrants have been non-white. The vast majority are Hispanics or Asians. Like all migrants since the dawn of humanity, they are strivers, doers and optimists, chasing dreams, escaping nightmares. They are lettuce pickers, chamber maids and drywall installers. They are nurses, software engineers and neurosurgeons. They've filled our labor force needs; swollen our ranks of small businesses and entrepreneurs; and helped keep our Social Security system afloat. They aren't all model citizens. But the vast majority are. In all comparative measures of criminal and other anti-social behaviors, immigrants (including those who are here illegally) fare better than native born Americans. We're lucky to have them.

Here's what Ronald Reagan said about immigrants in his farewell address in 1988: "Thanks to each wave of new arrivals to this land of opportunity, we're a nation forever young, forever bursting with energy and new ideas, and always on the cutting edge, always leading the world to the next frontier. This quality is vital to our future as a nation. If we ever closed the door to new Americans, our leadership in the world would soon be lost."

The modern wave of immigrants has done something more. It has created an American mosaic richer and more multi-colored than anything we or any other nation has ever known. Because of them, the United States is on course to become a majority non-white nation by the middle of the 2040s. In the process, our racial boundaries have become porous. Back when boomers came of age, interracial marriage was nearly non-existent – still illegal in a third of our states and a taboo everywhere else. Today nearly one in five new marriages is across lines of race. One child of such a marriage – Barack Obama – has already spent eight years in the White House. More will surely follow.

Big change provokes big reactions. Immigrants are an easy target, not just because they've changed the face of America, but because roughly one in four is here illegally – the result of weak border policies and business interests eager to preserve the flow of cheap labor. For the past decade, Trump has conducted a master class in how to exploit this issue for political advantage. When he first ran in 2015, immigrants were "bringing drugs, they're bringing crime, they're rapists." By 2023 they were "vermin" who were "poisoning the blood of our country." The awful rhetoric echoes Hitler but goes down well with his hard core MAGA base. Of all the reasons our political tribes are at each other's throats, immigration tops the list.

Here's a mash-up of marriage statistics that dramatizes both the change and the backlash. Newlyweds today are three times more likely to marry across racial lines as across party lines. Think about that. Amazing! America is more accepting of diversity than ever – and also more freaked out by diversity. Sometimes a thing and its opposite are both true at the same time. This is the dizzying, disorienting place where the boomer crusades of the 1960s have deposited our country half a century later.

By my reckoning, the MAGA crazies are on the wrong side of history. But I can't let progressive boomers off the hook. Over time, as our focus shifted from individual rights to group rights, our moral crusades too often devolved into purity campaigns and DEI excesses. And too often they were waged with an elitist disregard for the travails of the working class.

The 2024 election was a cage match between these opposing boomer strains. Both candidates were boomers – Kamala Harris, 60, just old enough to qualify; Trump, 78, just young enough. She embodied the social revolutions of the past half century; he embodied the backlash. The backlash prevailed, by a narrow but decisive margin.

So too did our modern era gerontocracy – in defiance of our heritage and history. On Inauguration Day, 2025, 82-year-old Joe Biden turned over the office to 78-year-old Donald Trump. They are the two oldest men ever elected president – this at a time when the median age in Congress is also at a record high. During her short-lived campaign against Trump for the 2024 GOP nomination, former South Carolina governor and U.N. Ambassador Nikki Haley described Congress as "the most privileged nursing home in America" and called for mandatory mental competency tests for elected officials over the age of 75. Like her candidacy, her proposal went nowhere, even though a 2023 Pew survey found that that 79% of Americans supported age limits for federal elected officials.

In early 2026, Barack Obama weighed in on the gerontocracy: "I'm 64 now. I'm pretty healthy. Feel great," he told a podcaster. "But the truth is, half of the references that my daughters make about social media, TikTok, et cetera, I don't know who they're talking about. At some point you age out, you're not connected directly to the immediate struggles that folks are going through. I'm not making a hard and fast rule here, but I do think that Democrats do well when we have candidates who are plugged into the moment, to the zeitgeist, to the times, and the particular struggles that folks are thinking about as they look towards the future rather than look backward toward the past."

History is on his side. America was founded by audacious young men. In 1776, James Monroe was 18, Alexander Hamilton 19, John Marshall 20, James Madison 25, John Jay 30, Thomas Jefferson 33, Thomas Paine 39, John Adams 40, and George Washington 44. For the past decade we have been led by stubborn old men who have not aged well in office.

I wish I were more confident that today's younger generations will lead us out of the morass. I *am* hopeful that, one birth and one death at a time, some of their most attractive values will prevail. There's nothing that today's young prize more highly than diversity, be it racial, sexual, gender, religious. For much of American history, "melting pot" was the aspirational metaphor for a nation of immigrants. For the America of today and tomorrow, it's "mosaic." The young don't aspire to look and act like everyone else. They celebrate differences. They want to protect individual identities. Good for them.

I'm less confident that they will embrace other values needed to sustain a healthy multi-cultural democracy. Our public square has become such a dark place, we have normalized so much bad behavior, we have made hating-the-other so much of a partisan badge, we have tolerated so much economic inequality, that it's hard to imagine there won't be a lasting impact on the attitudes and behaviors of the generation raised inside this civic hellscape. Even though most of my beef is with the reactionary right, I also worry about the folks on my side of the partisan divide, especially the young. On college campuses, inside social media echo chambers and across multiple outposts of popular culture, they are growing up as a liberal generation with illiberal tendencies – a victim mentality, an intolerance of viewpoint diversity, a distrust of institutions, a wariness about human nature, a cynicism about the whole American experiment, an instinct for group aggrievement at the expense of national identity.

Democracy is sustained by a thousand small sanities. It depends on civic habits that need to be learned, re-learned and maintained by muscle memory. "Democracy is one of the most faith-fueled human activities there is," writes author and citizen activist Eric Liu. "It only works when enough of us believe it works. It is at once a gamble and a miracle."

Historian Thomas Bender has written: "Nations are, among other things, a collective agreement, partly coerced, to affirm a common history as a basis for a shared future." In his famous novel, *1984*, George Orwell wrote: "Who controls the past controls the future: who controls the present controls the past."

In our age of discontent, Americans are fighting with each other about all of the above: the past, the present, the future. The battle lines are as much by generation as by party. No matter what their political affiliation, most boomers take pride in the official version of American history. We're the greatest nation on earth, with noble ideals and, yes, messy realities. Today's young have been raised – by their teachers, their culture, the wisdom of the streets – to focus mainly on the mess, especially those stemming from our original sins of slavery and racial oppression. Nearly nine in ten boomers say they're very proud to be Americans. Just a third of young adults say the same.

It's tempting to compare today's turbulence with that of 1960s. Yes, there was a lot of crazy stuff going on back in the day, especially on campuses. But there's one huge difference. Back then, 72% of 18-to-24-year olds told pollsters that, even though they might oppose the Vietnam War or disagree with other policies, they trusted the government to do what's right most or all of the time. Now just 14% of young adults tells pollsters the same thing.

Love of country can be a dangerous elixir. So can its absence. Three decades ago the philosopher Richard Rorty said that the progressive left will "help to make our country much more decent, more tolerant and more civilized…But there is a problem with this left: It is unpatriotic…It refuses to rejoice in the country it inhabits. It repudiates the idea of a national identity, and the emotion of national pride."

His admonition feels timelier than ever. Today's America is trying to become a nation the likes of which the world has never known: a multi-racial, multi-ethnic democracy in which no one group is in the majority and in which the blessings of political, social and economic liberty are shared by all. We'll get there only by heeding the founders' motto: E Pluribus Unum. Out of many, one. We'll get there only if today's young understand that a mosaic needs more than its beautiful and varied pieces. It also needs glue.

That's the new American Dream. The boomers started America on this journey, then too many chose to pull up the ladder behind them. We created a winner-take-all culture that triggered a populist discontent that empowered a Me Generation boomer-in-chief to lay waste to our youthful idealism.

Trump says he will make America great again. An ancient Greek proverb says: "Societies become great when old men plant trees whose shade they will never sit under." For most of our history, we've been a nation of planters: the transcontinental railroad, the Interstate Highway System, the internet, land grant colleges, world class universities, the Erie Canal, the Hoover Dam, the Tennessee Valley Authority, the NIH, the Marshall Plan, NATO, a sturdy social safety net, a mighty military, a beacon of hope to people everywhere who yearn to be free.

Today, the symbol of our government isn't a beacon. It's a wrecking ball, a chainsaw, a masked para-military thug. Down this path lies a lesser America. My deepest hope is that younger generations will find their voice and mount a revival. I don't know how or when this will happen. Can't happen soon enough! As for my generation, it's too late for do-overs. Our ledger is full, our time nearly up. The Grateful Dead had our number, way back when. Long, strange trip.

CHAPTER THREE

IN THE BEGINNING

Growing up, Stefanie was quite something. Many somethings. By the time she was twenty, she had been a tom boy. A viola player. A lifeguard. A twirler. "Football Queen" and "Cutest Girl" at James Madison High School in Brooklyn.[9] A telephone receptionist for the Circle Line in Manhattan. A tour guide at the state capitol in Albany. A social worker. A member of SDS[10] who peed on the Pentagon at one anti-war demonstration ("There were no Port-a-potties!") and got arrested for civil disobedience at another demonstration on her SUNY campus in Albany. A college drop out. A Woodstock reveler.

I knew her for some but not most of those adventures. Our mothers – Bea and Phoebe - loved telling the story of how we met. It was 1952. We were each three years old. When they saw us playing

---

[9]   *Alma mater of Bernie Sanders, Chuck Schumer, Ruth Bader Ginsburg, Norman Coleman, Chris Rock, Carole King, Judge Judy, Martin Landau, Mad Magazine founder William Gaines, five Nobel Prize winners and my mom.*

[10]   *Students for a Democratic Society, the leading "new left" voice of the Sixties.*

together in our summer community in upstate New York, the two of them allegedly burst out in unison: "Wouldn't they make a lovely couple!"

Newsrooms have an acronym for anecdotes like that: TGTC. Too Good to Check. If fiction, so what? Fact is, I vividly remember being smitten by young Stefanie when we were six or seven. She had big green eyes, golden hair and a perfect little pony tail. Whether our little gang was climbing trees, skipping rocks or hurling ourselves off rafts, she was always in the thick of the action. I was on the periphery. Most of the parents in our community were school teachers. My parents weren't, so they didn't have their summers off, which meant that I didn't spend nearly as much of my childhood up there as she did. Throughout our teenage years, I didn't recall seeing Stef at all.

Fast forward to the summer of 1969. I'm 20 years old, in between my junior and senior years in college. I have a summer job as a reporter for The Saratogian in Saratoga Springs, the racetrack-and-resort town 20 miles south of our community in Lake Luzerne. As usual, my parents have rented out our cabin. I'm living right next to it, in a motel-unit-sized mini-cabin that my grandparents had plunked down a decade earlier when they realized that my neat-freak mom and her scattered-brained mother couldn't coexist in the same kitchen. Stefanie is living by herself in an apartment in Brooklyn. She'd dropped out of college and has a job as a social worker's aide at Maimonides Hospital. She has a boyfriend in graduate school at Stanford. Her parents don't approve. That spring they tried to talk her out of flying across the country to visit him. After much yelling and screaming, she reassured them as she headed off to the airport, "Don't worry. If the plane crashes and I die, you're forgiven for everything you just said."

Their spat was short-lived, as they always were in the Teitel household. In July, Bea phoned her. "Come up and visit Daddy and me at the lake. Do you remember Paul Taylor? He's here this summer. He's beautiful."

That motherly match-making pitch became a source of much merriment among Stefanie and her co-workers at Maimonides. Stef spent the next few weeks musing theatrically: "When should I go upstate to meet beautiful boy? What should I wear when I meet beautiful boy? How should I act when I meet beautiful boy?"

Later that month Stefanie did come up. We bumped into each other one afternoon on the path to the lake. I was coming, she was leaving. I was tongue-tied. Made stupid small talk. Handled myself like an oaf. Mercifully, the encounter was brief. Later that night we bumped into each other again, this time in a mutual friend's family cabin. It was July 20, 1969, the night of Neil Armstrong's moonwalk. A bunch of us gathered to watch the live television feed on a small, grainy, rabbit-eared black-and-white TV – one of the few sets in the community back then. The room was crowded; Stefanie and I were sitting on the floor. She was wearing a Mexican blouse, shorts and sandals with straps that went halfway up her legs. At one point as she reached for a bowl of potato chips, one of her legs brushed up against one of mine. Karma? Cosmic signal? Accident? ("Honey," she later clarified, "it was no accident.")

The next day we hiked to nearby Rockwell Falls, clasping hands as we maneuvered over the rocks. The next weekend I drove down to the city to visit her. We kissed for the first time at the top of the Empire State Building. Right away, we both knew. I was unencumbered but Stefanie had some loose ends to tie up. She needed to untangle from her Stanford boyfriend (about whom more later). And she needed to put up with some razzing at Maimonides. "I had to tell everyone that, yeah, well, oops, it turns out beautiful boy is kind of cute."

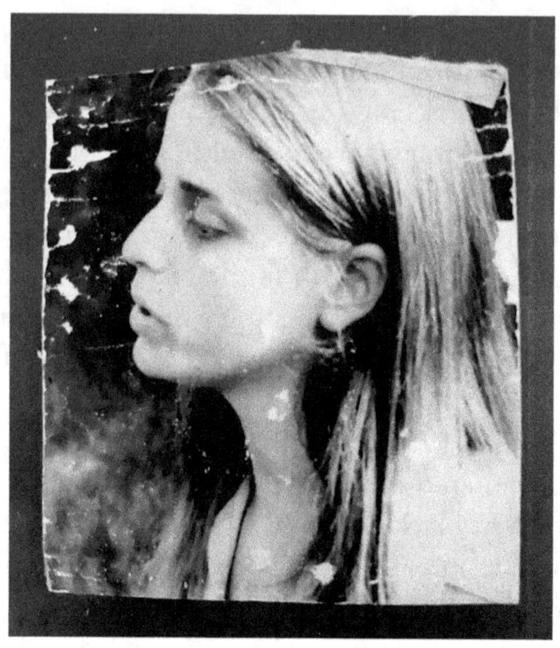

I took this photo of Stefanie in 1969. It's been in my wallet ever since.

I think you would call us an unnatural match. Stef was passionately anti-war and hard left. I was moderately anti-war and center left. In normal times, this wouldn't amount to a hill of beans in a romance. But the late 1960s weren't normal. America was aflame with civil rights, women's rights, gay rights, assassinations, urban riots, campus protests, Vietnam, Earth Day, Woodstock, sex, drugs and rock n roll. We baby boomers were in the thick of it, all of it. In 1967, Time magazine named our generation its Person of the Year, a journalistic bauble typically reserved for presidents, popes and assorted pooh-bahs. Seemed about right to us. We were going to save the world.

Stef and I needled each other over our political differences; we didn't try to convert each other. She likes to tell the story of a Saturday in New Haven when there was a huge anti-war demonstration headlined by Bobby Seale, he of Black Panther and Chicago Eight fame. "I go to the Bobby Seale rally and fucking Paul goes to watch his roommate row crew!"[11] Despite her displeasure that afternoon, she found other things about me to like. Early in our relationship, she remembers the two of us driving on a highway late at night and coming upon a black man on the shoulder standing next to his broken-down car. "You hit the brakes, jumped out of the car and asked if you could help. And I remember thinking, 'Hmm, this is a pretty good guy.'" Half a century later, I have zero recollection of that incident. (These days I have zero memory of nearly everything. Just wait, kids, it'll happen to you too!) But apparently it left a lasting impression on the object of my desires.

I do remember this: my lovely, lusty, vulgar girlfriend had no end of charms. She was a sponge, a life force, a free spirit. "Not a bit tamed," to borrow a line from Walt Whitman. During my senior year in college, each Friday night when I met her at the train station in New Haven, she could barely contain herself with stories about all the *amazing* things that had happened on the train ride up from the city. Once we got to the beach house I was renting in East Haven, we'd head straight for the bedroom, where storytelling would quickly give way to sex. We'd giggle a lot. We'd make other noises. This did not amuse my sex-deprived Yale roommates, one of whom had a girlfriend in California, the other in Pennsylvania. At some point during our festivities, they'd bang on our paper-thin bedroom wall, screaming "Stop it! Stop it!! Stop it immediately!!" – their mock indignation

---

[11] *Stefanie is a connoisseur of the word fuck. Out of her mouth, it conveys a dazzling range of emotions: amazement, anger, surprise, disappointment, resignation, approbation, skepticism, disapproval, indignation. She enjoys shocking people with it, especially men she's meeting for the first time. Marking her territory. And by the way, she honed her skills when "fuck" was as transgressive as you could get. Like everything else, profanity evolves. Among today's young, the f-word is barely taboo. Believe it or not, scholars track such things. It's been nearly two decades since fuck made it into the top ten list of offensive words, according to an annual survey of college students conducted by Benjamin Bergen, a professor of cognitive science at UC San Diego and author of What the F.*

braided with carnal envy. Which of course produced more giggles on our side of the wall.

During our year of courtship, I came to realize that my hippie girlfriend had plenty of traditional values. The little girl whose parents warned her that she'd get a blinding headache if family dinner didn't start at the stroke of 5:30 p.m. had outgrown that fear by the time we met, but she was still a devotee of structure, order, punctuality and, above all, family. Yes, she had her skirmishes with her folks over the usual stuff – boys, curfews, school work. But these were battles, not wars. She and Norm once went for a couple of weeks refusing to speak to each other. (Norm: "Someone please tell Stefanie to pass the salt." Stefanie: "Please tell Daddy the salt is on the way.") Stef can't remember what the row was about. In any event, it left no scars. "My thing was to deflect, not confront. I was pretty good at staying out of fights with my folks and just doing my own thing."

It helped that Stefanie's politics were a badge of honor in the Teitel household. Norm and Bea were lefties too. When Stef got arrested at SUNY-Albany for picketing campus recruiters from Dow Chemical, manufacturers of napalm, Norm wrote a scathing letter to the college dean demanding to know why the university police had called the Albany cops rather than act *in loco parentis* in support of his daughter. Norm and Bea drove up from Brooklyn on the day of her trial for disorderly conduct. On the advice of her lawyer, Stef had come to court dressed in the white blouse and blue skirt uniform she wore as a tour guide at the state capitol. "Right before the hearing starts, my parents show up and my mom is wearing big earrings with bells that literally jingled," Stef recalls. "My lawyer looks at me and says: 'Your mom?' I say, 'My mom.'" The judge reached his guilty verdict in the blink of an eye.

Bea, Norm and Stef with her peace lapel pin.

Left-wing politics, traditional family values, loving cross-generational vibes – that's a pretty good bumper-sticker summary not just of the Teitel family but of our whole summer community. It was founded in the early 1920s by Jewish school teachers from Brooklyn. Most were children of Eastern European immigrants. They had young families and free summers and big dreams, and they yearned for a respite from the heat of the concrete jungle. Anti-semitism was rampant, so they also wanted a place where they could vacation among their own. They created it on a pristine, uninhabited lake in the foothills of the Adirondacks, 50 miles north of Albany. It's the fourth in a chain of small lakes that empties into nearby Lake Luzerne, and just beyond that, into the Hudson River. Thus the oddly banal name for such a jewel: Fourth Lake.

Our magical lake

My grandparents Max and Rose Weiss were among the first settlers. Max taught math and was an assistant principal at Cunningham Junior High, which Stefanie would attend years later. In the 1920s dozens of other Brooklyn school teachers and their families bought or built small cabins at Fourth Lake. Back then it took two days to make the trip up from the city, but the lure of clean air, dirt roads, cool nights and sweet well water was irresistible. They quickly created a flourishing summer colony that revolved around square dancing, folk dancing, duplicate bridge, a community newspaper. They organized music, art and dance lessons. They conducted study groups for teachers who were preparing for licensing exams. After World War II, a second wave of summer settlers arrived, among them Norm and Bea Teitel. In the 1950s, with Fourth Lake experiencing its own baby boom, the community created a day camp for us kids. For two hours every weekday morning, our parents sorted us into different age groups and gave lessons in swimming, boating, hiking, tennis, music, arts and crafts, wood-working and star gazing. And just by the way they led their lives, they handed down lessons that weren't in the day camp curriculum. Throughout our entire childhood, there was just one divorcee among the more than 50 families in Fourth Lake (and she got divorced three times!) The take-away was impossible to miss. Marriage really is till-death-do-us-part. Stef and I took that guidance to heart. Our contemporaries, not so much.

By the early 1950s the community had organized itself into an association with elected leaders, by-laws, a board of directors, a dozen committees, initiation fees and annual dues. In 1952 it purchased 30 acres of land and created a private beach on the south side of the lake. In the 1960s, it built a community house. There's always been a utopian quality to life in Fourth Lake that carries echoes of the kibbutz movement in Israel – the optimism, the social solidarity; the belief in the power of collectivism. Like the kibbutz founders, nearly all of us are Jews – in our case, proud but mostly secular. In keeping with the customs in our branch of the tribe, we've done a lot of "marrying out" over the years.

In Fourth Lake, political ideology rivals religion as a source of community cohesion. That was especially true in the early years. From the 1930s to the 1950s, some Fourth Lakers were drawn to communism, which enjoyed a boomlet within the American left throughout the Great Depression and on into World War II. After the war ended and the horrors of Soviet-style communism were laid bare, most of these "fellow travelers" let go of their youthful enthusiasms. In our summer community not all did. If you're a student of the Red Scare, you may be familiar with the rallying cry: "Who Promoted Peress?" It referred to Irving Peress, an Army dentist who served in the Korean War and had received a routine promotion from captain to major despite being under surveillance for having ties to a U.S.-based Communist front organization. When Irv refused to name names and invoked the Fifth Amendment a dozen times during his 1954 testimony before Congress, Sen. Joe McCarthy branded him "a Fifth Amendment Communist."[12]

Irv eventually got an honorable discharge, but he and his family endured years of hate mail and harassment, much of it antisemitic. His home in Queens was stoned; his wife had to give up her position with the local PTA; members of his daughter's Brownie troop were warned against the dangers of subversion. Decades later in an interview with the *New York Times,* Irv answered McCarthy's question. The culprit, he said, was bureaucracy. "You know who promoted me? Somebody was eating lunch or making a telephone call when my promotion passed across their desk. I slipped through." When he died in 2014 at the age of 97 he got a big obit in the New York Times. A few days later The Times ran a letter-to-the editor with one of my all-time favorite headlines: *My Leftist Dentist.* "It was something of a point of pride to have your gums examined by someone who had been persecuted by Sen. McCarthy," the letter began. "He was a great dentist. To this day I use unwaxed dental floss and Oral B soft toothbrushes because that's what he recommended. Rest in peace, Dr. Peress."

---

[12]   *At another hearing later that year, Army lawyer Joseph Welch grew indignant when McCarthy lobbed a similar accusation at one of Welch's young colleagues. "Let us not assassinate this lad further, Senator," Welch thundered from the witness table. "You've done enough. Have you no sense of decency, sir?" That cri de coeur, captured live on broadcast television (then still in its infancy), marked the beginning of the end of McCarthyism.*

By the time I got to know Irv, he was a quirky old man.[13] He was intrigued with me because I covered politics for the Washington Post. We sometimes jousted over current events, but always with a twinkle. He hadn't changed his mind about anything. "Regrets?" he had told the Times when he was in his eighties, "No. None at all. True believers don't have regrets." But at that stage of his life, he was ready to take everything down a few notches. Not all of Fourth Lake's aging fellow travelers spent their elderhood on the same gentle glide path. Saul Kamen was still wearing his "Fuck Capitalism" lapel button into his eighties, even as capitalism was proving most accommodating to his four hugely talented and warm-hearted sons, all of them dear friends to Stef and me.

Norm and Bea were close to the Kamens and the Peresses. They weren't fellow travelers, but they knew their way around the neighborhood. They sang the praises of the literacy programs in Castro's Cuba. So did other Fourth Lakers of their generation. But not my parents.

My dad viewed communism as an affront to humanity on a par with fascism. At various points in his life, he led local chapters of the Liberal Party and ACLU, which made him a lefty in good standing everywhere except among the lefties of Fourth Lake, where he was a source of curiosity, even suspicion. For five years in the mid-1950s, he had been a junior diplomat in the State Department, stationed first in Japan and then in Vietnam. In Stefanie's eyes, this made him a creature of the evil establishment and – who knows – maybe a spy. Over time, as she grew more impressed with his absent-mindedness, she gave that theory the burial it deserved.

---

[13]   *Irv relied exclusively on the Times for his news consumption. Toward the end of his life, battling a range of health issues, he had trouble keeping up. He would stack the unread papers on his porch and read them when he could, always in chronological order. One summer I bumped into him on the beach and asked where he was in time. "Late May." "Hey, you're in for a treat. We've had a run of good news lately." "Don't spoil it for me."*

In the early years of our marriage there was low-grade tension between the two of them. Dad was put off less by Stefanie's politics than by the trappings of the counterculture she wore every day – T-shirt, jeans, no bra, aviator sunglasses. Oddly, the sunglasses seemed to bother him the most, especially when she wore them indoors. Dad liked seeing people's faces (hmmm, CIA?). The two of them sparred regularly over Vietnam. These arguments energized Dad, who loved nothing more than a big dust up over politics, philosophy, ethics or morality, but infuriated Stefanie. Their encounters usually ended with a cease fire (sometimes with my nudging) before they got too raw. Once we started having kids, their relationship thawed and eventually warmed. Stefanie's sterling qualities as a mother could melt the heart of any grandparent.

And then when the unimaginable happened – when my mother killed herself – they grew close. Stef came to see Dad less as an annoying adversary, more as a lost and vulnerable soul. It was Stef who mentored my dad in how to manage a kitchen, a car, a household – realms that my mom (and his mom) had kept off-limits to him. The breadth of dad's cluelessness about the hum-drum of life never ceased to amaze us. Dad didn't know that cars needed oil as well as gas. He didn't know that a frozen chicken needed to be defrosted before it went into the oven. He didn't know that a half-eaten can of peas belonged in the refrigerator not the cabinet.

But there were many things Dad did know, and many more he sought to know. He was a child prodigy who graduated college at age 19 and spent the next six decades searching for the meaning of life. In his voluminous essays he set forth many certitudes. The most important thing is to love and be loved. Nearly as important is to strive, compete, do you damnedest. Reason is what separates humans from lesser life forms. In the pursuit of a worthy life, reason is the most reliable guide – far superior to emotion or faith.

Dad harbored a lifelong grudge against God. It started when, at age 12, he was introduced to the story of Abraham in Hebrew class.

It struck him as the ultimate cruelty. What kind of God commands a man to kill his first born – and does so not to test his love of God, but his fear of God? He went ahead with his Bar Mitzvah the following year, but in protest refused to repeat his speech at the traditional family celebration dinner that evening.

Dad kept up his beef with the Almighty right until the end. He spent the last decade of his life seeking a publisher for "The Case Against God," a powerfully argued, deeply researched screed that he wrote after he had earned a late-in-life PhD in philosophy. His book never found a publisher or audience. This left him frustrated but not despondent. Dad marched to his own drummer. He had strived, he had done his damnedest, he had applied his considerable intellect to the most fundamental questions. For him, the search for meaning was the meaning.

But when it came to some of his certitudes, he wavered at the end. He was shattered by mom's suicide. He never forgave himself for not being more in tune with her needs when she fell into what turned out to be a fatal depression. He never got beyond his grief and guilt, though over time they grew less all-encompassing. He lived for another twenty years, eventually remarried and led a reasonably happy life. But the light was gone. And gone, too, was his belief that we are all the masters of our fate. Mom's death led him to write a series of essays about predestination. He had always acknowledged that there are mysteries in the universe beyond human understanding. Now he went further. Perhaps everything is predetermined – all part of a grand design we mere humans have no way to comprehend, not even through the power of reason. Maybe that's why his beloved Phoebe killed herself.

⌣

Dad never saw it coming. One afternoon he came home from tennis to find their apartment empty. He called out for mom. No answer.

He searched all the rooms, Nothing. Eventually he made his way to the bathroom. The door felt heavy as he pushed it open. Then he saw why. Mom had tied a belt around her neck. She was hanging from the towel hook on the inside of the door, her feet dangling a few inches above the floor.

Dad was 63 years old, about to retire from his job as a trade association executive and about to receive his PhD in philosophy (dissertation title: "Liberty and Equality in the Social Order"). Mom was 58. She was an employment counselor and for many of her clients, a beloved life coach. She was the author of "How to Succeed in the Business of Finding a Job," a self-help book for people making career transitions. She was active in several women's professional associations. She and dad had been married for 37 years. They had wonderful friends. They had two happily married sons and three adorable little grandchildren. Their golden years beckoned: travel, tennis, golf, bridge. For Dad, more time to write essays and think big thoughts. For Mom, more time to romp on the floor with her grandkids.

Then the unthinkable.

Dad never figured out why. Nor did I. Not then, not later, not ever. The horror itself, I remember only in fragments. I was in the kitchen of our house in Philadelphia when the phone rang. It was dad, which was odd, because it's always mom.

"Mom's gone," he said in a voice so soft I could not make out his words.

"What?"

"Mom is gone. She's dead."

"What? What?? What??? What happened?"

"She killed herself."

I remember slumping to the floor. I don't remember anything else about the phone call. I don't remember how I got from Philly to DC that night. I do remember arriving at my parents' apartment and seeing someone I had never seen before. It was Dad, except he didn't look like Dad. His athletic frame seemed to have collapsed in on itself. He was frail, shrunken, in shock. He spoke in a flat whisper and told me things that night I had never known. Twenty five years earlier, Mom had suffered a depression that led to a hospitalization and electroshock therapy. For all her warmth, wit, energy, and joie de vivre, Dad said, she struggled all her life with self-doubt. Recently she had fallen into another depression. But Dad had no idea how bad it was. No idea.

All of this was almost as unfathomable to me as the act itself. Mom was "the greatest mommy in the whole wide world," as I loved telling her when I was a little kid. She was the warmest, liveliest, funniest, most cheerful, most loving person I knew. Because of her – and because of Dad too – I had the happiest of childhoods. She told me I could be anything I wanted to be when I grew up. I believed her.

I was 30 years old when she committed suicide. No longer a child. How could I have been so blind to the dark side of her life? And why did I cut short our last phone conversation? She had called two days after the mayoral election in Philadelphia, which I'd covered for the Philadelphia Inquirer. I was swamped working on a bunch of follow-up stories for the Sunday paper. After a few minutes of chit chat, I said, "Gotta go; let's talk Sunday." My last words to my mother. Half a century later, they haunt me still.

Dad was so distraught and ashamed that he insisted we tell no one beyond family and close friends that Mom's death had been by suicide. For everyone else, it was a sudden stroke. I hated the edict but went along. Dad needed support and loyalty from his sons. Several years later, when he was about to remarry, I insisted that he tell his future wife the truth. He agreed. My stepmother eventually let me know that she knew, but we never talked about it. And once the shock finally wore off, Dad and I almost never talked about it. He wrote about Mom. He wrote about his guilt. He wrote about the mysteries of fate and the power of predestination. But he had spent a lifetime repressing his emotions. He wasn't about to start confronting them now.

Death ends a life but not a relationship. Suicide even more. It has been nearly half a century. I still don't understand. I've cycled through various phases: angry with Mom; angry with Dad, angry with myself, angry with everyone. I long ago gave up assigning blame. I wonder if the mad impulse was triggered by a bad reaction to a blood pressure drug she had begun to take (Dad, in shut-down mode, never pursued this line of inquiry). I also wonder if Mom had an undiagnosed bipolar disorder. Not long ago I read something written by the late actress Carrie Fisher that resonates: "Living with manic depression takes a tremendous amount of balls…if you're functioning at all, it's something to be proud of, not ashamed of. They should issue medals along with the steady stream of medication."

Stefanie often talks about the strength it must have taken for my mother to hide her demons from my brother and me. She's also haunted by an argument she and Dad had in 1972 when Sen. Thomas Eagleton was forced to step down as George McGovern's running mate after it was disclosed that as a younger man he had received electro-shock therapy for depression. Dad approved; he said no one with that medical history belonged on a presidential ticket. Stefanie was appalled; she said depression was a treatable disease, like any other. The saddest part of the memory: Mom had sided with Dad.

This was a different era. To my parents' generation, depression was a character flaw, a source of shame, best kept in the closet. People who struggled with the disease were often adept at masking the symptoms. Anti-depression medications were not yet widely prescribed. As I think back now on my childhood, I realize that there were several episodes – Mom's absence for a week; Dad's decision to cut short his tour as a diplomat in Vietnam and bring the family back to the States – that weren't the result of the reassuring cover stories my brother and I had been fed at the time. Children are wired to believe their parents. Mom was determined not to share her troubles with us or anyone else. Only Dad knew about them, but he didn't know how to help her cope with them.

After she died, he coped by writing lovingly about her. "You were the giver in our relationship and I was the taker. You valued me far beyond my worth. I was lucky beyond compare to have you at my side. You were a gem and I sparkled in your reflected light. Our personalities were very different. You were outgoing, bubbling and friendly, but tended to be fearful and unsure of your capacities. I am reserved, calm, steady, somewhat cerebral, with an inner self-confidence that you could not find, although you had every reason to feel it. We complemented each other. I needed your warmth, your wit, your nurture and your belief in me. You needed my affection, my loyalty, my pride in your accomplishments and my appreciation of all you did for me. You verbalized your feelings, I kept mine in check. Each of us responded to the needs of our nature...

"Suddenly, meaninglessly, you are gone, and an abyss of loneliness has opened in front of me. I may heal eventually, but I will never be whole again. Part of me will always be with you, in whatever place you are."

"Grief is praise," the author Martin Prechtel has written. "It's the natural way love honors what it misses." Dad spent the rest of his life grieving Mom. So have I. Grief-stricken, stumped, unable to find closure. Nearly half a century later, here's what I know: My happy childhood wasn't a mirage. My parents' happy marriage wasn't a charade. It was all real. So was the tragic ending. I'm sad beyond measure that my kids never got to know her. I console myself with imaginary scenes of the fun they would have had. The laughter. My God, the laughter! Mom would sometimes start laughing midway through her own jokes. Her face would turn red. She would gasp for breath. This would make all of us start laughing. Which in turn would take her laughter up to such hysterical levels that she had no chance of making it to the end of the joke. But she didn't have to. There could never be a punch line as funny as this.

I miss her. I'll always miss her. I have no idea why she killed herself. Maybe she didn't want to grow old? Could be. I don't know.

(L to R) Bea, Dad, Norm and Mom in Fourth Lake with their grandsons Ben and Jeremy. Two years later, Mom was gone.

CHAPTER FOUR

MORE THAN A WRINKLE

December 5, 2019

Dr. Peter Gehlbach, the top retina specialist at The Johns Hopkins Hospital, doesn't have much of a bedside manner. He'd been all business a year ago when he explained why Stef was not a good candidate for surgery. "You can probably find doctors willing to take this on. But the odds are lousy. And if it doesn't work, you could lose all the vision in that eye." We'd been referred to him because Stef had been diagnosed with a "retina wrinkle" in her left eye. Gehlbach told us that it might stabilize on its own. "If it doesn't and you keep losing vision in that eye, come back. We'll take another look."

We're back. The wrinkle hasn't stabilized; it's gotten worse. "If I use my left eye only, everyone I look at is in the witness protection program," she tells the doctor. "All I see is a gray blob in the middle." Gelbach already knows this. He has the results of her latest field test on his computer screen, along with images of her retina. He also knows that this is Stef's "good" eye, the one less impaired by the glaucoma that has been shrinking her peripheral vision for the past decade.

Glaucoma is a progressive disease with no cure. Stef has had dozens of surgeries to try to keep it at bay, but it just keeps coming. So glaucoma is constricting her vision in both eyes from outside in, and the retina problem is blurring her vision in one eye from the middle out. All of which is driving her brain and nervous system crazy – though, like clever worker bees, they keep trying to find ways to compensate. But their work-arounds may be contributing to Stef's other big health issue. She's a runner – seven miles a day, every day, rain or shine, for nearly 50 years – who can no longer run. Lately, she's been having trouble walking. Her gait is jerky, her arms flail, she sometimes tilts right or left. Her circuitry seems to have gone bonkers.

We've spent the drive up to Baltimore gaming out the decision we expected to have to make. "Suppose the doc says there's a 50/50 chance that the surgery will work—do we go with it?" Stef is no stranger to eye surgery, but all her previous operations have been relatively low risk. Their only objective has been to slow down the damage from glaucoma; there's never been any prospect of improving her vision. The retina surgery would be different. It might actually help her eyesight get better. But it would also be risky – "like trying to peel scotch tape off wet tissue paper," as one of her doctors had put it. We arrive at Hopkins never having worked out our tipping point. Stefanie says she's sure of just one thing: "If I lose all the vision in my left eye, I'm fucked."

Gehlbach takes the decision out of our hands. He says because of the damage Stefanie has already sustained from her glaucoma, he's not willing to do the retina surgery. "I've seen it too many times. When someone has your symptoms, the operation can go great, but the patient never gets her eyesight back. I often get called in after fact to try to clean things up. But you can't."

We're both taken aback. "Help me out doctor," I ask. "You say the glaucoma would screw up the recovery. Is it also what caused the retina wrinkle in the first place?"

"Nope, completely unrelated."

"You gotta be kidding!"

"Completely unrelated. It's as if you had the measles, then you broke your leg."

"Jesus," I say.

"Fuck," says Stefanie.

Gehlbach offers a sympathetic smile. He says if we want to go ahead with the operation, we could find doctors who would do it. But no, he won't. He also suggests it might be time for Stef to think about a cane or a guide dog.

The drive back to Bethesda is grim. Stef starts taking stock of all the ways her body has betrayed her. In addition to her eye problems and her movement issues, she's been dealing with neuropathy, osteoporosis and cirrhosis. Then something happens that almost never happens. She starts to cry.

"I'm fucked. I'm totally fucked. And by the way, buddy, you're fucked too. You should head for the hills. I'm serious. This is going to be really, really bad. You should get out while the getting's good."

I'm no good at comforting my wife. My go-to words of wisdom in times of trouble – "This too shall pass" – have long since been reduced to a family punch line. Turns out being congenitally upbeat doesn't wear well. I try a different tack.

"I'm not going anywhere," I say quietly. "And yes this sucks."

The tears soon dry up. Stef takes a stab at gallows humor. "I guess I don't have to worry about gaining weight," she says, contemplating life as a blind person. "I'll eat whatever I want. Spend all day in bed, having sex. I'll make buttered popcorn with warm caramel. Whaddya think?"

"Sounds pretty good."

But of course nothing sounds good. It is a very sad drive home. On top of everything else, we know what's waiting at the end of the ride. Stef's mom is about to die.

Bea Teitel is a month past her 96th birthday, several years deep into dementia and two days into hospice care. She and Norm were both public school educators and lifelong New Yorkers. Four years ago, when their health began to crater, their minds began to play tricks on them and their personalities curdled, we moved them into a retirement home near us in Bethesda. Last year, when they flunked out of independent living, we moved them into an assisted living facility. Three months ago, after Norm died, we moved Bea into a secure dementia wing for residents who need what's euphemistically called "memory care." That's where she is now, sleeping 20 hours a day, unable to eat, getting fed a steady diet of morphine through a dropper.

Stef is a care giver by nature. An earth mother. Looks after everyone – her kids, her grandkids, her parents, me. Over the years our house has been a landing pad for plenty of strays – children of friends; friends of children – who were in some sort of transition or crisis and needed a place to crash. Sometimes days became weeks, even months. Hard to leave with Stef offering her understanding ear, her old soul wisdom, her great meals. Plus a washer and dryer that didn't need to be fed with coins.

But by her own lights, she's failed abjectly at being her parents' care giver. It eats away at her that after seven decades of marriage, at a time when they should be basking in the glow of lives well-lived and progeny well-launched, Bea and Norm have instead spent their golden years paranoid, delusional, angry, frightened, bickering and relentlessly unhappy. And she can't fix them.

Mercifully, Bea isn't in pain. Norm wasn't either. Another blessing: through all of the fog and all of the crazy, they've always known who their family members are, though sometimes only with prompting. And they've never turned on any of us, the way Norm turned on nearly all of the surpassingly patient aides who have looked after them in their later years.

Norm was the sweeter spouse, dashingly handsome, generous, warm, empathetic. Bea has more drive, a restless energy, sharp elbows. She is quick to judge, she's a bit of a snob, she resents other people's money, she enjoys telling people how they ought to be living their lives. Especially her children and grandchildren, though if the opportunity presents itself, strangers too. When she was in her 50s, she got her PhD in education. Had she done that when she was younger she could have used the degree to climb the hierarchy in the New York City public school system. She had the smarts, skills and temperament for leadership. But she left the profession for a long stretch to raise her kids. So she spent her career as an elementary school teacher, and eventually a teacher of teachers. As near as Stef and I could figure it, the most tangible reward she got from that late-in-life PhD was the pleasure she took in identifying herself as "Dr. Teitel" whenever she made a restaurant reservation. "Mom, what happens if you're in the restaurant and someone gets sick and the manager calls out for Dr. Teitel to please come help?" Stef used to tease her. "You're screwed."

Norm and Bea were a union of opposites. They had a rock solid marriage, but things began to crater when they were in their late eighties. Norm, always more laid back than Bea, began to slow down dramatically. His naps were lasting most of the afternoon. He was having trouble finishing his thoughts. He was mangling the punch line of jokes he'd told a thousand times. He was prone to wacky conspiracy theories. Bea took all this in with scorn rather than sympathy. She'd shoot him a snarky dig. "Norman, get to the point!" Privately she would confide to Stef: "There's something wrong with Daddy. I'm telling you, he's not right in the head." Stef would tell her, "Mommy, it's not Daddy's fault. He's getting old. Why do his naps bother you?

What's he keeping you from doing?" "Nothing!" Bea would reply, loudly, angrily, haughtily, defiantly. "I just don't want him sleeping all day!"

Norm – sweet, gentle Norm – eventually started barking back. He was in his early 90s when for the first time ever I heard him raise his voice to her. Both of them by then had outlived their inhibitions and their grasp of social conventions, so they sometimes had their squabbles in front of the kids and grandkids. Family celebrations were bittersweet. On their 70th wedding anniversary, I toasted them for 65 years of wedded bliss. (The attempt at drollery flopped). That same year at the end of an unsettling Thanksgiving dinner with all their children and most of their grandchildren, we attempted an intervention of sorts. We sat them down in our living room and one by one told them how much we loved them and how much they needed to cut the crap. Two of their granddaughters suggested marriage counseling. Norm and Bea listened silently, morosely. They put up no defense. They sat at opposite ends of the room like naughty kids who knew they'd done wrong but had no intention of changing. I think they knew they couldn't change. They were captives of the new people they had become.

Things never got back to normal between the two of them. At the very end, however, the late-in-life marital bile finally dissipated. This happened when Bea's own confusion had come into full flower. On one of our last visits with the two of them, after Norm finished one of his rants about God-knows-what, Stef asked Bea what she thought. This time, no eye rolls, no embarrassed shrugs, no schoolmarmish scolding. "Daddy is very smart," Bea announced. And that was that. In their 73rd year together, peace and harmony had returned to the marriage. Happiness, no.

We decide not to visit Bea the afternoon we got back from seeing Gehlbach. We're both emotionally fried. The last thing Stefanie needs is another session at Grand Oaks. Over the years she's found it more and more unbearable to visit her folks. Starting well before their retirement home years, she watched with mounting sadness as their social orbits kept shrinking. Nearly all their old friends have by now passed away. Norm and Bea never made any new friends – – unwilling, unable, probably both. They never took up new hobbies or interests. Despite relatively good physical health, their world has grown smaller, angrier. Stef hates that she can't fix them. She worries that she'll become them. Still, she visits three or four times a week. And because she can't drive, I often go along. Our visits are brief. Almost by ritual, they end with Stef reciting the same mantra as we head for the parking lot: "Just shoot me."

I'm not nearly as traumatized. I'm sad for them, of course, and even sadder for Stef. But I'm also fascinated by the randomness of their wackiness. What mischief the brain makes when its wires get crossed! Every time we drive over there, Stef and I would ask each other: "What surprises do the happy couple have for us today?" Would Norm fly into a rage about the aide who made his bed the wrong way? Would Bea carry on about the mysterious strangers who've been sneaking into the dining hall and stealing all the food? When would Norm get hauled back into the principal's office? In one recent episode, he had reduced an aide to tears by parking himself and his walker in front of the apartment door and refusing to let her leave. Her offense? As near as we could untangle it, he was furious that she hadn't said a respectful goodbye. "Daddy, you really can't do that. It's sort of like holding someone hostage." Norm shrugged, unconvinced, unrepentant.

In early September, Norm went into hospice care following an infection. He was sleeping nearly 24 hours a day. It was clear the end was near. One afternoon Stef said to him: "I know you promised Mommy you would always take care of her. I know you're too tired now and I know how upsetting this must be for you. But don't worry, we will all take care of her. And we all love you."

She had no way of knowing if he heard her or comprehended what she was saying. The next day he passed away peacefully, in his room, with Bea by his side.

We weren't sure how much Bea comprehended. For the following few days, she was flat, inert, uncommunicative. No expressions of grief. No tears. She would periodically ask Stefanie where Daddy was. When Stef asked if she understood Norm had died, she said yes. But she seemed puzzled.

On the third day she asked Stef, "How come Daddy died?"

"He got sick, Mommy. And he was old. More than anything else, he wanted to take care of you until the very end. But his body gave out on him."

"How old was he?"

"96."

"That's old! How old am I?"

"You're almost 96."

"96?? I thought I was in my 70s. 96 is old!"

The next day Bea was more coherent than she'd been in a long while. "I've figured out my problem," she announced after we wheeled her onto a balcony on a balmy autumn afternoon. "I've lived too long. It's time for me to die. But here's my real problem and believe me it's a big one. I don't know how! I suppose I could try to jump out of a window or off the balcony. But I don't have the strength."

Stef let her words sink in. "We're only on the second floor, Mom. You might hurt yourself but not kill yourself. Wouldn't that be a mess?"

Bea isn't about to be dismissed with dark humor. She tells Stef she's serious.

"Well, if you're serious you could stop eating," Stef says. "That's supposed to be a painless way to drift away."

Bea ponders the idea for a moment. "Aren't we having filet mignon tonight?"

Go figure.

⌒

But we can't figure. We have no clue what's going on inside her brain. We move her into the memory care wing so she can be monitored more closely. In the next few weeks there are more green shoots of the feisty old Bea. With Norm no longer around to wage war, she gets along well with her new aides. She mentors Stacy, an immigrant from West Africa, on the distinction between "lay" and "lie." She offers relationship advice to Ivy, whose boyfriend isn't ready to get married. "You're a smart lady. Tell him if he doesn't marry you, you're moving to New York and getting a job at one of the hospitals there. Tell him he needs to shit or get off the pot." Ivy loves telling Stef and me that story. Bea does too.

But she keeps toggling between feisty and crazy. She's in full battle cry against the crime syndicate that's been stealing her clothes and selling them on the street. "Big scam. You have no idea. Don't get involved. Too dangerous." She wonders why the staff is preventing her European friends from visiting. (She has no European friends). She accuses the woman down the hall of stealing a necklace that had gone missing a decade earlier in New York. "I was all set to grab it, but she was too fast. She ran away." Not clear what part of that story was loonier – the idea that the woman had stolen her necklace or that either of them was ambulatory.

⌒

A month or so before she died, Bea surprises Stefanie with a question. "How come you're so good to me? I was never very good to you." Stef doesn't know what to make of this. With the end near, is her mother seeking forgiveness? For what? Stef isn't inclined to go there; she doubts Bea is in any condition to go there either. "Mommy, you've always been great to me," she says, bringing the exchange to a swift and compassionate close.

Bea was always a loving mother and wife, but rarely a warm-hearted one. Maybe that's what she was trying to say. Over the years Stef would sometimes complain with mock angst that her mother liked me more than her. Like most family jokes, this one didn't come out of nowhere. Bea was status conscious. She was also a newspaper junkie. My career as a Washington Post reporter and occasional TV talking head was a feather in her cap. So yes, we got along just fine. In the weeks before she died, I have my own odd encounter with her. She's very pleased with the way I've arranged the furniture and hung the art and family photos in her new room in the memory care wing. After thanking me, she adds in a tender voice, "You know, Paul, I've always thought of you as my second…." I return her affectionate gaze as I wait to hear that I'm like a second son.

"…husband."

Whoa.

Toward the end of November Bea grows much more frail. She can no longer prop herself up in her wheelchair – her body droops, her head tilts. She's hospitalized briefly for pneumonia. The folks at Grand Oaks let us know she's ready for hospice care. In the ensuing weeks, everyone in the family visits and says their goodbyes. Most of the time, Bea is uncommunicative or asleep. But she seems at peace. She is not in pain. The morphine helps. Stef and I keep our visits short. Stef is not one for bedside vigils. She has no scores to settle, no unfinished business to tend. Deep down, I hope she knows she'd done everything she could.

We get the phone call at 7 a.m. on a Monday morning. After Stef hangs up, we embrace for a very long time. We are overcome with sadness. Even more, with relief.

Bea and Norm in Fourth Lake

Parents teach their children about living and then, at the end, they teach them about dying. From the way her parents lived, Stefanie learned to be a worrier. She learned to be frugal. She learned that everyone is entitled to a fair shake.[14] She learned to be skeptical of human nature and distrustful of institutions. She learned to be a champion of equal rights and a friend of the underdog. She learned that family is the center of the universe.

From the way they died, she learned that that's not how she wants to make her exit. Her just-shoot-me's give way to a more sober conversation between the two of us about the end of life. We agree that her folks had lived too long for anyone's good, especially theirs. They'd spent their last chapter shutting themselves off from the world; shutting themselves down. Those retirement homes near us were full of active elders eager to make new friends. Eager to keep living. Norm and Bea couldn't/wouldn't go there. Toward the end they started taking meals in their room rather than risk social interaction in the dining hall. Stef would encourage them to get out. Norm would assure her: "Don't worry, it only costs an extra $7 to have a meal delivered to our room."

They had made a loving but fundamental miscalculation. They'd managed their lives on the tightest of budgets so they wouldn't wind up as a financial burden on their children. At this, they succeeded. We used their nest egg to finance top-of-the-line care in their last years; for that, everyone in the family is grateful. But the ironies were poignant. They never found a way to enjoy the fruits of their frugality. Meantime, they did become an emotional burden, especially on Stef. They never saw that coming. By the time it happened, it was too late for them or anyone else to do anything about it. We agree that if either of us were to get to that point…well, neither of us is going to let the other get to that point. So we'll write up our DNRs. We'll let our

---

[14]   *Whenever they broke out the pistachio nuts during long car rides, Norm and Bea would make sure Stefanie and her siblings counted out their portions, nut by nut, so that no one got shortchanged. Another food-related ritual: The three kids had to take blind taste tests before Norm and Bea would agree to stick with high-priced brands like Heinz ketchup and Hellman's mayonnaise. "If we couldn't tell the difference, we'd have to go back to the generic store brand. But we could always tell the difference!"*

kids know that lying helpless in a memory care unit isn't for us. Our end-of-life directive: "If in doubt, snuff me out."

Reasonable? Sure, but reason doesn't always get the last word. Once all the relatives disperse and our house empties out, Stef falls into a deep funk. Actually, she's been in and out of funks for several years. How could she not? Now, on top of everything else, she's still in pain from a fall she took when she caught one of her flailing arms on an electric pole guidewire she never saw. She tore her meniscus on the way down, requiring surgery and a few weeks on crutches.

A few days before Christmas, at around 4 a.m., she limps back into bed from the bathroom. She can tell that I'm awake.

"I'm so tired of being me," she says. Our bedroom is lit up by a gorgeous full moon shining through the skylight. I can see the most defeated expression I have ever seen on my wife's beautiful face.

"I want out. Really, I just want out. I'm ready to end it. I'll feel bad about you, but you'll do fine. You'll be a great catch. I'll feel bad about the kids, but they'll do fine. Maybe I'll leave them a note. They need to know how much I love them. But I think they already know."

I'm lying alongside her in bed, in silence. Stefanie has talked about killing herself before, but this feels different. More ominous.

She says she doesn't want to make the trip to New York City to be with our sons and their families during the Christmas holidays. She doesn't want to go to Philadelphia to be with the same gang of friends we've hung with on New Years Eve every single year since 1976. She doesn't want to do anything at all. "I just want out," she says. "I just want out."

A thousand bad thoughts bounce around in my brain. I have no idea what to say. I lie there, petrified. Finally I wrap my arms around her. "We're going to get through this," I tell her. But I'm not sure.

CHAPTER FIVE

WE HAVE A PLAN

January, 2020

The holidays come and go. Stefanie gets through them okay. The worst of her blues have passed, but things are still pretty dreary. And I still can't figure out what to make of her talk of suicide. I'm virtually certain that she doesn't really mean it. That she would never act on it. Day in and day out, she's functioning well, so it seems clear she doesn't have classic symptoms of depression. But what if I'm wrong? What if my this-too-will-pass optimism has led me to misjudge the peril? If I were to make my father's mistake, I could never forgive myself. And never stop grieving. Trouble is, even if I decided I needed to do something, I wouldn't know what to do. I'm not good at this. If these dark ruminations were coming from anyone else, I'd know exactly what to do: Ask Stefanie.

Four years later, as I was writing this section of the memoir. I did ask Stefanie. Here's what she said:

"You knew – and if you didn't know, you're an idiot – that I would never do that to you and the kids. I was saying something different – something I've thought about my entire life, not just in bad moments like that one. And it's simply this – if a person can no longer take care of himself or herself, they should be free to decide if they want to keep on living.

"Different people have different thresholds. We've had friends – my parents had friends –who have been faced with very difficult choices. Some have said, enough, no more, I'm done. Others have said they want to carry on. I'm totally okay with everyone's choices. I just want to be able to make mine.

"I'm at a point in life when I think about the stuff I can no longer do. I'm a very visual person. I can't make jewelry any more. Yes I can still take walks, but I can't see the trees. And when I walk, I sometimes look like a fucking drunk.

"This is all probably going to get worse. If it does, I know you and the kids will take care of me. But I don't want that. I don't want to be a dependent person. That's not who I want to be. That's not the life I want to lead.

"So no, I would never spring anything on you. But if I ever get to the point where I feel like I'm below my threshold, we're going to have to have a talk.

Stefanie is not the only one feeling the blues. I'm having my own bouts too. Four years into Trump's America, I feel like a stranger in my own country. I keep having to scrap so much of what I thought I knew about human nature, political behavior, the national character. How could so many of my fellow Americans fall for this odious man? Such a depressing question, especially for a congenital optimist and American chauvinist. I'm even having trouble paying attention to the news. It's overflowing at the moment with stories I would normally devour – impeachment hearings underway in Congress; the presidential caucuses gearing up in Iowa – and yet for the first time in my life I can't make it through the morning papers.

Clearly we both could use some sort of reboot. Travel would be the obvious choice, but Stef's vision problems have made that less appealing. She's uncomfortable in unfamiliar places.

The solution is hiding in plain sight: It's the house in Fourth Lake we've just inherited from Norm and Bea. We've known for years that it would pass down to us after they died, but we've never figured out what we'd do with it. We already have a cabin up there – the one I took over from my dad after mom died; the one where our kids (and now their kids) have spent nearly all their summers. So now we'll have two houses, a couple of hundred yards apart. A family compound! Kids, grandkids, siblings, cousins, aunts, uncles all spending the glory days of summer hanging out together in our little slice of paradise.

It seems idyllic. But there's a catch. While there's a lot we like about the Teitel house, there's a lot we don't like. That's why we haven't known what to do with it. Now that it's ours, and now that we're in the market for some sort of grand adventure, we hatch a plan: Lets fix, change or get rid of every damn thing we don't like. Turn it into our dream house. Our gift to ourselves, our kids, their kids, eternity. As we start talking about the million changes we'll need to make, Stef is more animated than she's been in months. Actually, years.

When people like us decide to renovate a home, they typically hire an architect and a contractor and then spend the rest of the project writing checks and worrying about cost overruns. Not us. We're a little weird. We do it ourselves. If you add up all the additions and renovations we've done in multiple houses (ours and our kids) over many decades in multiple cities, the tally is pretty mind-boggling: 17 bathrooms, six kitchens, six bedrooms, three decks, two porches, two laundry rooms, a workshop and a study. It's pretty much the only activity (other than the basics – kids, friends, sex) we do together as a couple. We don't have the same hobbies or interests. I play sports and I'm a big sports fan; Stefanie doesn't and isn't. I follow politics obsessively, once for a living, now as a recovering junkie; Stefanie doesn't. She reads voraciously, she runs (or walks) six miles a day; she cooks, she used to make jewelry, pottery and stained glass. All solitary activities. I traveled a lot for work, but we haven't traveled much as a couple. We assumed there'd be plenty of time for that once I retired.

Do-it-yourself home renovation has been the comfort food of our marriage. We make a terrific team. We have similar tastes and eyes, so the planning has always been stress-free. And once the actual work begins, there's been a natural division of labor. Stefanie manages the project, pays the bills, purchases the materials and hires the subs when we need them. She also does all the tiling (we use a lot of tile!) and, until she started to lose her vision, all the painting.

The family raises a wall on the addition we built in 1986 to the Fourth Lake cabin I inherited from my folks.

I do the grunt work. I learned my carpentry skills—such as they are, and they aren't much – from Norm. He built the cabin we've just inherited. Stefanie's brother Lee was his right-hand man. Stef, her sister Beth and I all pitched in. I was 24 years old and barely knew one end of a hammer from the other. Norm taught me how to use a power saw, how to frame a wall, how to hang a joist, how to set a nail, how to miter an edge, how to string a staircase, how to mix concrete, and how to do scores of other stuff, big and small, simple and complicated – just by letting me watch him. His father had been a carpenter, but Norm was mostly self-taught. His parents didn't want him to make a living with his hands. That's not why they'd come to the land of opportunity. They wouldn't let him touch his father's tools. Naturally, this piqued young Norm's curiosity. He would sneak peeks whenever his dad was doing a project in their apartment. After his dad died, Norm took up carpentry as a hobby. And in 1973, when a prime parcel of land that overlooks the creek between Fourth and Third Lakes came up for sale, he embarked on the grandest carpentry project of his life. He would build his dream house in a magical spot surrounded by pine trees that soar 120 feet toward the sky, overlooking a creek that meanders through the forest.

With the help of a nephew who was getting his architecture degree, Norm and Bea came up with a dramatic design: an L-shaped wooden structure, two stories high, with steeply-pitched roof lines; an interior balcony overlooking a large living room; a handsome stone fireplace; floor-to-ceiling glass walls and a spacious rear deck overlooking the creek. It was nothing like the other cabins in the community. With just a few exceptions, they were modest, one story, Adirondack-style summer cottages. This was an immodest mid-century modern vacation home. It was also completely out of character. Norm and Bea were children of the Depression. They led frugal lives; they colored inside the lines; they were risk averse. But Bea had just gotten a $15,000 settlement from an injury she'd suffered falling down an apartment house staircase. The windfall put them in an un-characteristically expansive mood. Against their nature, Norm and Bea shot for the Moon. I think it may have been the boldest thing they ever did.

It was also a hugely enjoyable family project. I took an immediate liking to home construction. Producing something tangible every day rings my bell; it's one of the reasons I became a newspaper report-er. Plus, a piece of me has always wanted to be an architect. I don't have an artistic bone in my body, but I have strong feelings about form and function. Stef calls me the "architect Nazi." Our neigh-borhood in Bethesda has become a hotbed for mansionization, and when we take our evening walks, I'll stroll down the streets muttering: "Nope." "Nope." "Nope." "Nope." To my eyes, the neo-Tudors, faux chateaus, colonial revivals and boxy moderns look extravagantly dif-ferent and depressingly similar. Oversized structures on undersized lots, crammed together like bottles of perfume on a display counter, trying too hard to impress.

We get a thumbs up from everyone in the family when we tell them about our idea. So Stefanie and I start brainstorming. This is usually the most enjoyable part of our DIY projects. The inevitable hassles of execution are still off in the distance. For now it's all blue sky – time to let the imagination roam free. But oddly, right from the get-go, there's a low-grade tension between us.

We argue about how to fix the greatest design flaw: the house has no dining room. Norm and Bea thought they didn't need one. They were mistaken. Big family meals were the liveliest part of life in the Teitel household, but they had to be staged with everyone cramped around a crowded kitchen table. Getting to the seats along the far wall was like fighting your way down the aisle of an overbooked air-plane. Once you arrived, you'd better be prepared to stay for a while.

Because Norm, from his perch at the head of the table, enjoyed lingering over his food. After dessert, he'd still be chomping away on stray husks of corn. If you were sitting along that far wall, your escape route was blocked. But it wasn't just the folks in the cheap seats who suffered. Everyone did. Because while we were all squeezed for hours around that kitchen table, that gorgeous living room sat empty, out of sight, out of mind. Might as well have been in another zip code.

Stefanie and I have no trouble agreeing that the obvious solution is to build a dining room inside the L formed by the kitchen and the living room. It would have an open floor plan. We would remove the two walls on the inside of the L and build a new room with wide open lines of sight to both the kitchen and living room. So far so good. But we disagree on the shape of this new dining room. Stef wants a standard rectangle. I propose something more daring – a triangle. Rather than build two new walls inside the L, I want to build just one – a hypotenuse. It's an idea that's been marinating in my head for decades.

"The traffic flow and the sight lines will be fantastic," I announce over breakfast in Bethesda. "You can be working in the kitchen and still be in eye contact and carry on conversations with people in the living room. We'll line up the dining room table alongside the angled wall. There'll be plenty of space around it. The two halves of the house will finally be in harmony."

Stefanie isn't buying it. "There won't be enough room for a table. And it will look ridiculous. Way too modern. It's an Adirondack cabin, not a Colorado ski chalet."

"It already looks like a ski chalet. Nothing we can do about that. But we can open up the flow and get the sight lines right."

Stef is in a surly mood. Suddenly she's all over me. "You're going to do whatever you want. That's what you always do."

"Really? Aren't we too old to have this fight? How about we chill?" That's me in passive aggressive mode. It never goes well.

"Of course you want me to chill. Then you'll do exactly whatever the fuck you want. You always do."

"Not true! I only get my way on stuff I really care about. All the other stuff – which is actually the vast majority of stuff – you do whatever you want."

"That's only because the stuff I want doesn't piss you off. This will piss me off."

"Look, we can't work this out here and now. We need to go up there, measure the rooms, get out some graph paper, put some tape down on the floors and see how everything lines up. Then we can decide."

Stefanie accepts the cease fire. We'll settle this another day. The encounter has been unnerving. But every moment we're fighting about rectangles versus triangles is a moment we're not thinking about how many things in our lives have gone to shit. Maybe the plan is working.

A few weeks later I come up with another plan.

I'll ditch the idea I'd been mulling over to update my last book. Instead, I'll write a book about renovating our cabin. A book about a long-married couple fighting loss, decline, health problems, old age. About generations and family. About our hundred-year-old community. About retreating from a world that no longer makes sense. About passing the torch; leaving a legacy; choosing renewal over despair.

This would be outside my comfort zone, and quite possibly, my skill set. I'm an observer of others, an explainer of trends, not a chronicler of self. Never done anything like this. And what's my motivation? Glory? Narcissism? Self-aggrandizement? None of that fits with the person I like to think I am.

Then there's the problem of putting our personal lives on public display. Stefanie has always said there should be a special place in Hell for politicians who use their family members as props in their campaigns. How is she going to feel about her husband using her as the lead character in his coming-of-old-age memoir?

Gingerly, I raise the topic with her. I make it clear that if she's not okay with it, this idea dies right here. I assure her that she'll read every word in advance and she'll have absolute veto power. Stefanie listens carefully. Her reaction surprises me. Rather than objecting to the invasion of her privacy, she says she can't imagine why anyone would want to read that book.

"Will you be disappointed if no one publishes it?"

"Sure. You know my favorite quote – – no man but a blockhead ever wrote, except for money. Too damn hard."

"But why would anyone want to buy it?"

"I think we're sort of interesting people. And at the moment, our problems are kind of interesting. Might make a good story."

"Famous people can get away with writing about their lives and their problems. No one is going to find our lives interesting."

"Well, I think you're interesting. You. My wife"

"I'm not interesting."

"Actually, a lot of people find you interesting. Plus, you're having interesting problems. Your health issues are interesting."

"Lots of people have health issues much worse than mine."

"Yeah. But you're a medical mystery. None of your doctors can figure out what's going on. Are your eye problems and your movement problems connected? Makes a good story."

"You're my husband. You're biased."

"How about we let the marketplace decide? Who knows if this book ever gets written, much less published. But if it does, we can let the market decide if your life is interesting. Meantime, you ok with me going ahead?"

"Sure."

"And you're okay if I write that one reason we're doing this renovation is to get you out of the funk you're in?"

"So basically this book is going to be: 'We're fixing up this house so my wife won't kill herself.'"

Before I can think of something to say, Stef rescues me. She tacks in a different direction.

"Maybe you should give me a pseudonym. How about Esmerelda?"

"Okaaay. But what good would that do? The people you care about will know it's you. As for everyone else, who gives a shit?"

"I guess that's right. Who gives a shit."

With that, Stefanie acquiesces. I know she thinks this a bad idea, not just because she doubts anyone will read it, but because she doesn't want me making a spectacle of our problems. Her problems. But there's something else I know. Stef has never stood in the way of me doing what I wanted to do. She's often been pissed off about the demands of my job, especially those long reporting trips when the kids were young. And she'd let me have it. "If you stay out for more than a week, buddy, don't bother coming back." But we both knew that was theater. Stefanie loves me. She wants what's best for me. Always has. When I write this book, I'm gonna need to make sure the reader understands that.

She also knows a thing or two about leverage. One night as we were getting into bed after an evening in which she'd listened to me describe the book to our daughter and son-in-law, Stefanie gave me a not so gentle warning.

"You're not going to describe me as a neurotic crazy person, are you? Because I'm not in for that shit."

"Of course not."

"And because you do want to get laid?"

"I understand the stakes."

CHAPTER SIX

THE LIFECYCLE OF HAPPINESS

I used to walk like an athlete. I used to *be* an athlete. Pretty good football and baseball player in my youth. Very good tennis player, especially as I got older. My tennis game peaked at the unlikely age of 60, the year I won the Maryland State 60-and-over men's singles championship. (The tournament draw happened to be weak that year. But still). If through some miracle of time travel my 60-year old self could have played a match against my 20-year old self, it would not have been pretty. That kid was extremely quick and had a big topspin forehand. But he'd spent his childhood running around his pitiful backhand. A fatal weakness that mature and wily me would have mercilessly exploited. I'm thinking 6-2, 6-2. No contest.

And what about now? How would 77-year-old me fare in this imaginary Paul Taylor Time Travel Invitational? Well, he wouldn't be playing. When I was 66 I ruptured my right quad tendon in a freak accident on a golf course.[15] And when I was 72, I ruptured my left quad tendon on a tennis court – another freak accident! Two surgeries and countless rounds of physical therapy later, I walk like an old man. The closest I get to competitive tennis these days is when I turn on the TV.

Me at batting practice at Vet Stadium in Philly in the 1970s. (My rec league team had arranged access to the field for the day). Half a century later, I sorta think I'm still that guy.

---

[15] *My three-wood shot from the fairway has settled in a bed of hickory nuts on the sloped fringe of the green. I'm pumped. This is a par five; I'm there in two and thinking chip, putt, birdie! I pay no attention to the peril lurking underfoot. When I step on those hickory nuts, they behave like ball bearings. I take a spectacular fall. My knee dislocates; my tendon ruptures. Never got a chance to go for that birdie.*

It's weird that I obsess about this, but what can I say? I'm one of the boomers I make fun of – the kind who thought he would stay young till the clock ticked all the way down to zero. In fact, if you asked me right now how old I feel, and if I chose to answer the question honestly (knowing I'd make a fool of myself), I would tell you: My knees feel like they're about 120 years old. The rest of me is 24. Okay, maybe 36.

Call this what you will: vanity, insanity, narcissism, nostalgia, nuts. All of the above. But it turns out that even though I'm a hard case, lots of people my age suffer from the same delusion. When I was at Pew, we did a big survey about aging. One of our findings was that the older people got, the wider the gap between their actual age and their "felt" age. The vast majority of twenty- and thirty-somethings said they felt very close to their actual age. But among respondents my age, one in three said they felt between 10 and 20 years younger than their chronological age, and another one-in-six said they felt more than 20 years younger than they actually are.

"It's bizarre, if you think about it," Jennifer Senior wrote in an essay about this phenomenon for The Atlantic. "Certainly most of us don't believe ourselves to be shorter or taller than we actually are. We don't think of ourselves as having smaller ears or longer noses or curlier hair….Yet we seem to have an awfully rough go of locating ourselves in time. A friend nearing 60 recently told me that whenever he looks in the mirror, he's not so much unhappy with his appearance as startled by it – 'as if there's been some sort of error,' were his exact words."

Exactly. *Some sort of error.* That's how I feel every time my birthday rolls around. Can't we get a recount? There's something wrong here. As for looking in the mirror, I had the weirdest experience maybe 20 years ago. As I prepared to shave one otherwise uneventful morning, the person looking back at me wasn't me. It was my mother. Mom!!! Good God you and I have the same face. Never noticed that before. Startling.

Surveys taken all over the world have found that this perceptual age gap among older adults is greatest in the United States, Western Europe and Australia, and that it has been growing wider in recent decades. Researchers mostly attribute it to a crude form of denialism, old age being a club most of us are not eager to join. But as Senior notes, "You could just as well make a different case: that viewing yourself as younger is a form of optimism, rather than denialism. It says that you envision many generative years ahead of you, that you will not be written off, that your future is not one long, dreary corridor of locked doors."

Many gerontologists share this view. "We know that those who feel younger are healthier," says Markus Wettstein, a psychologist at Humboldt University of Berlin. "They also remain healthier over time." Research shows that older adults who feel young at heart not only tend to live longer, they have more life satisfaction, lower dementia risk and fewer depression symptoms. It's not clear what's the horse and what's the cart, but there's no doubt they go together.

All of this raises a question: If more older people are feeling ever younger, how does this square with the premise of this book: That getting old sucks?

Before I take a stab at an answer, I should acknowledge that these aren't the only data findings that undermine my cranky premise. In the past few decades there's been a boomlet in social science research about the lifecycle of happiness. As the PhDs will all tell you, there are many ways to measure happiness. But no matter how they ask the question or what population, nation or region of the globe they survey, their findings have been strikingly consistent. The lifecycle of happiness is U-shaped.[16] People tend to be happy when they're young and have their lives in front of them. They grow less happy in middle

---

[16] *In recent years, the left slope of the U has flattened out somewhat as teenagers and young adults in developed countries all over the world have struggled with anxiety and depression. More about this in Chapter 10.*

age, as life tosses its curve balls and the weight of work, family, finances and failed dreams bears down. But starting at around age 55, they get happier as they get older.

Happier as they rack up more aches and pains. Happier as their body parts sag; their hearing and eyesight deteriorate; their skin wrinkles. Happier as they lose hair, muscles, balance, bone density, brain cells. Happier as they can't remember where they left their keys, or the name of the actress in the movie they watched last night. Happier as the medicine cabinet gets more crowded, the doctors' visits pile up, the funerals too. Happier as people pay less attention to whatever they have to say. As I've already noted, if you stick around long enough, this is what's in store. So how come there's an upward arc in the happiness curve in the later stages of life?

One explanation has to do with the wonders of modern medical science, which have extended the number of years we live *and* the number of years we live in relatively good health. Gerontologists use a "frailty index" to measure the overall physical and mental health of elderly patients. Surveys and data analysis show an encouraging trend. The typical person who turns 75 this year will be one percent less frail than the typical person was when he or she turned 75 last year. And two percent less frail than the typical 75-year-old had been two years ago And so on. We haven't cured old age, but we're postponing it. Good news!

Even so, we're still left with the underlying mystery: How come we get happier as we get older? Everyone from philosophers to poets to social scientists to psychologists to religious leaders has taken a stab at an answer. If you forced me to distill all their wisdom into an overarching Theory of the Happiness U-Curve, it would simply be this: People adapt.

Yes, getting old sucks, but people adapt. They do this in a hundred different ways, and some are better at it than others. But most old people adapt well. Maybe they lower their expectations, throttle back on their ambitions, let go of old resentments, stop obsessing over life's disappointments; make peace with who they are, warts and all, and who they'll never be. Maybe they embrace new challenges, adventures, hobbies, purpose. Maybe they find new friends or partners. Maybe they smell the roses, hug the grandkids and feel grateful for all that's gone right for them in a world where so much has gone wrong.

Happiness in old age is different from happiness in youth. When a group of researchers analyzed the emotions that 12 million personal bloggers mentioned when they wrote about feeling happy, they found a striking pattern by age. Younger bloggers wrote about feeling excited, ecstatic or elated; older bloggers wrote about feeling peaceful, relaxed, calm or relieved. As social psychologist Heidi Grant Henderson has written, that's because as we grow older we shift from "promotion motivation" – seeing our goals in terms of what we can gain – to "prevention motivation" – seeing our goals in terms of avoiding loss and keeping things running smoothly.

There's another emotional skill that tends to sharpen as we get older – we get better at ignoring all the irritating little stuff because we've been around long enough to know that, ahem, this too shall pass. "This is almost like a superpower many older people have," writes happiness guru Arthur Brooks. "They know that negative emotions won't last so they get a head start on feeling good by consciously disregarding bad feelings as they arise."

Then, too, there's the simple mercy of making peace with yourself. "One of the blessings of age is that most of us get along with ourselves better than when we were young," writes Anne Lamott, a novelist and author of a guide-to-aging-well column for the Washington Post. "It is stunning to accept yourself: I am always going to have a womanly butt and now I appreciate it: It's a nice seat cushion."

Lamott also wrote about how, as we age, we're better able to grasp the miracles in everyday life: "That we are no one else but our very own selves is a miracle. About one hundred million sperm were released each time your parents made love, and one dogged little guy made you into exactly you, the exact being who woke up again today. Our eyes open, our ears open and, if they don't work that well, we have devices to help them. Our hearts are beating. Our lungs are bellowing in and out, our diaphragms rising. The muscles release and contract and get us up again. Sometimes we need others to help us. Both are amazing, the strength to rise or the loving help."

This is the wisdom and serenity that comes with age. Stefanie and I need more of it. We need to become better adapters. We need to smell more flowers. Our parents – much as we loved them – were not good role models. They did not age well. But it's not as if we don't have good role models. We have lots of them. And it's not as if we aren't coping with old age from a perch of enormous privilege. Of course we are. Which makes it all the more annoying that we aren't doing it better.

On the subject of role models, let me introduce you to Ben and Carol Beach. They've been dear friends and neighbors for 40 years. Our kids went to elementary school together. We've had hundreds of dinners in each other's homes. We've shared all the milestones, joys, sorrows.

When it comes to measuring his older self against his younger self, Ben doesn't need an imaginary time travel tournament. He's a marathon runner, and a famous one at that. He can simply compare times.

Ben ran his first marathon in 1968 as a freshman at Harvard. Until then he hadn't been a competitive athlete. But he'd run a bit on his own and, the year before, had happened to listen to a live radio broadcast of the Boston Marathon. The weather was miserable that day; Ben was intrigued by the crazy grit of the runners who braved those 26 miles. And as soon as he ran the race himself the following year, he was hooked.

He resolved never to miss a Boston Marathon. When he was in his 30s, he ran the race in under two and a half hours – seriously fast! At age 50, he was still completing the marathon in under three hours. And the streak had become an important part of his self-image.

But then things got weird. His walk remained normal, but whenever Ben ran, his left leg would get hijacked by erratic signals from his brain. Sometimes it would lurch off at wild angles. Sometimes it would drag. Sometimes it would clip his right ankle, causing him to trip. Ben consulted doctor after doctor. No one had a diagnosis, much less a cure. After four years of searching, Ben finally got an explanation from specialists at NIH. They told him he had an unusual neurological disorder known as focal dystonia – the yips – that has cut short the careers of many athletes, musicians, artists and craftsmen. They began treating him with a regimen of Botox injections in his left hamstring. By weakening that muscle, the injections make his leg less susceptible to the neurological chaos. But this is not a cure. Ben now runs with a severe, almost cartoon-like limp.

By the time he was in his 60s, the combination of the yips and old age left him struggling to run the marathon in under six hours, the cut-off time for a runner's performance to be recorded as official. But he kept running anyway, and that's how he got famous.

In 2017, at the age of 67, Ben became the first person ever to complete the Boston Marathon 50 consecutive times. I wrote an article about his iron man streak that year for the Washington Post. There was a lot of media coverage in Boston too. On the day before the big race, he threw out the honorary first pitch at the Red Sox game at Fenway Park.

It hasn't been easy. As he got older his grown kids started taking turns running alongside him for stretches of the race to keep his spirits up. He has a long-term running buddy who did the same thing. In addition to dystonia, he's had to fight all the slings and arrows that come at any marathoner – injuries, cramps, muscle pulls, bad weather. "When you think about it," he said. "I've been incredibly lucky."

His luck ran out in 2022. About six weeks before the race that year, he took a bad spill while training on his bike. He suffered a concussion, fractured his orbital bone and needed surgery to relieve swelling in his brain. After 54 years, the time had come. The streak was over.

"The risk was too great. I didn't want to put my family through it. The streak was an important part of who I am, so it was a really hard decision. But I've made peace with it."

Ben keeps himself in shape (he weighs exactly what he did in college, 125 pounds) and runs in a few shorter races every year. His times, he says, are "pathetic."

"When I was younger, I remember telling another runner that I couldn't imagine what it would be like to run an eight-minute mile. Eight minutes! Come on, that's not even running! Now I'm grateful that I can run a 13-minute mile."

Ben isn't the only adapter in the Beach family. Carol developed Parkinsons when she was in her mid-40s. Her symptoms were mild at first, and the progression was slow. But relentless. When she was in her late 50s, she underwent deep brain stimulation surgery, which has helped her to manage the symptoms.

"I used to say that if you're going to have a degenerative disease, Parkinsons is a good one," she told me in the fall of 2023. "I used to feel like I could outrun it. But it's catching up to me. I feel like I can't outrun it anymore."

Carol was once a terrific all-around athlete. When their kids were growing up, she coached their soccer teams, managed their baseball teams and refereed for their field hockey leagues.[17] That part of her life is long gone. In recent years she's been boxing with a trainer a few times a week to keep her muscles from freezing. But there are days when walking is a challenge. And there are days when her greatest joy – nannying for the grandkids – leaves her exhausted.

---

[17] *Ben and Carol's daughter Emily was a starter on the University of Maryland's national championship field hockey team.*

"When I was young, I had an aunt who told me that when things get bad, just remember, there's always someone out there who has it worse. I always try to keep that thought top of mind. But it's getting harder."

In November 2023 Carol fell down the stairs of their Bethesda home. She gashed her head, suffered a concussion and brain bleed, briefly lost consciousness and was taken by ambulance to the emergency room. She recovered, but her gait became even slower, her speech and balance more tentative. Ben and Carol decided it was time to sell the house they'd lived in for 40 years and move to.... where? An apartment? Retirement community? Independent living facility? With levels? To a warmer climate? Closer to the kids?

Eventually most of us will face that rite of passage. If we're lucky we'll be able to make our choices on our terms and timetables. Ben and Carol opted for closer to the kids – which in their case meant a condominium apartment across the river in Alexandria, Virginia.

Stefanie organized a bon voyage dinner party. The guest list consisted of the women (and their husbands) who'd been in a book club with Carol and Stefanie for nearly forty years. The group started when they all had young kids. It was the one night a month that the moms could kick back, escape from the crazy of child rearing, and speak unfiltered truths to knowing ears. There used to be a dozen women in the group. Two have since moved away. Another four have passed away. Their monthly get-togethers didn't survive Covid, but the friendships have. Two hours before the dinner party, one of the guests emailed her regrets. Her husband, who also has Parkinsons, had started some new meds; his blood pressure had just plummeted. He was not feeling well. She was so sorry. She was so looking forward to seeing everyone.

We had a lovely dinner. There were happy memories. Funny stories. Gag gifts.[18] Empty seats. This is how it goes. Yes, you can grow happier as you grow older. You have to work at it.

A month later, Stefanie and I visited Ben and Carol in their new condo. They hadn't quite finished unpacking the boxes or hanging the pictures, but the place seems great. The best feature: no stairs.

Still, it was a melancholy visit. Carol told us: "I was hoping things would get better with the move. But it feels like things aren't going to get better." Her balance and gait are more tentative than ever. She rarely goes outside because she's not sure afoot. She said she doesn't want to use a walker because "there's no going back from that." But she also described conversation she'd just had with her Parkinson's doctor: "He told me that when he sees an older person with a walker, he doesn't see a sad story. Just the opposite. He sees a brave person who's not giving up. He sees someone who still wants to get the most out of life."

You can get happier as you get older. You do have to work at it.

---

[18]   *I gave Ben and Carol visas that allowed unlimited border passages from Virgina to Maryland.*

CHAPTER SEVEN

I LOVED BEING A HACK

I spent 25 years as a newspaper reporter. A hack, in the lingo of the craft I still love. Reporters of my generation weren't supposed to become part of the story. But that happened to me three times, each pretty dramatic. As I look back on those episodes, I ask myself what I got right and what I did wrong. The sort of questions you think about when you get to be my age.

Let's start in the middle. It's 1992. I've just become the Washington Post bureau chief for Southern Africa, based in Johannesburg. South Africa is in the throes of a bloody and uncertain transition from apartheid to democracy. Great story. Which for me began with a bang.

On my sixth day in Africa, somebody tried to kill me.

I was covering a nationwide general strike called by Nelson Mandela's party, the African National Congress, to pressure the white apartheid government to hold an election in which blacks would be able to vote for the first time.

Another reporter and I were driving through a township south of Johannesburg when we were cut off by car full of *tsotsies* – young hooligans who prey on residents with little to fear from the police, who are despised in the townships and have no interest in controlling the crime that flourishes there.

Four teenagers leaped out of their car, hauled us out of ours, and demanded our keys and money. I could see that at least one had a gun. The tsotsie who yanked me from the passenger side was a baby-faced kid of maybe 16 or 17. As hooligans go, he seemed to be on the likable end of the bell-curve. I made it abundantly clear that I was eager to oblige. Before I handed him my money, I showed him my press card. I wanted him to know I wasn't a cop, or some other agent of the hated white apartheid regime.

But we never finished the transaction. On the other side of the car, Phillip van Niekerk, one of South Africa's leading investigative journalists, was having a much rougher time. One of the young thugs clubbbed him over the head; another ripped off his jacket. One shouted: "Get out of the townships, motherfucker." Then he shot Phillip in the head.

The gunshot distracted my assailant, so I was able to walk around the car and try to help Phillip, who was on the ground with blood streaming out of his face. The shooter was hovering over him, gun in hand.

I got to within maybe eight feet of them. The shooter looked up at me; I at him. All I remember about his face was the rage. I also remember thinking: "Stay cool. Don't provoke. Either he's going to shoot you or he isn't. You'll find out soon enough." Then I felt an enormous punch inside my chest.

Winston Churchill once wrote, "Nothing in life is so exhilarating as to be shot at without result." He got that right.

The 9mm bullet tore a hole through the humerus bone in my left shoulder – without breaking it – grazed my lungs, smashed a rib in my back, then ricocheted harmlessly toward my breastbone – without breaking it – rather than a few inches in the other direction toward my heart. I fell to the ground, wiggled my toes and fingers and looked up to see a beautiful blue sky. I knew instantly I was going to be fine.

Phillip's luck was even more miraculous. He had been shot at point-blank range. The bullet entered his head just behind the right ear and exited just in front of his left ear. Astoundingly – and by fractions of an inch – it managed to miss both the top of his spine and the artery to his brain.

After the tsotsies sped off in their car and ours, there was a minute or two of eerie quiet. Then a crowd of township residents started to come out of their shacks. We were quite the spectacle: two white guys bleeding profusely in the middle of a dusty intersection in the middle of a black township in the middle of a patch of the world seething with suspicion and hatred.

This is a place where life can be scandalously cheap, where blacks get axed, speared, machine-gunned and "necklaced" to death – almost always by other blacks – for the affront of commuting to work, or attending a funeral, or having some money, or not taking part in a rent strike, or being a member of the wrong gang, faction, tribe or political party. It's also a place where white skin usually connotes cop, which in turn connotes state-sanctioned repression, torture and terror.

Was anybody in this outpost of hell going to help us? I still had my press card in my hand. I held it aloft and explained that I was a journalist, just arrived from the US, here to report on the horrors of apartheid.

I got blank stares in return. I wasn't sure why. I was a newbie in the country. I didn't know if they understood what I was saying. I wasn't even sure if they spoke English. As more onlookers arrived, I went through my spiel again. Meantime Phillip was screaming: "My God, I'm going to bleed to death. Somebody help!"

Finally, a voice emerged from the crowd, "We must help them." In a flash, the mood changed. This will always be my favorite example of how crowd behavior can turn on a simple nudge. Someone produced a car and drove us to a nearby clinic.

The attack on Phillip and me was front page news in South Africa and the United States. Two days later, I got a phone call in the hospital from our savior, a computer technician who had been in a nearby *shabeen* (tavern) when he heard the gunshots.

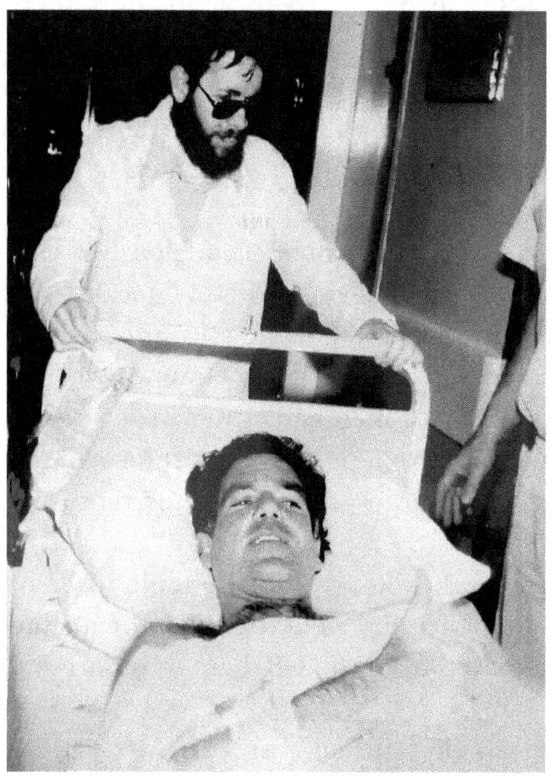

A Reuters photo of me at a Johannesburg hospital being wheeled into surgery to have the bullet removed from my back.

"Do you know what they were going to do to you?" Felix G. asked.
"I didn't have a clue. But until you showed up, it didn't feel good."
"They were going to necklace you."

That's the signature method in the townships for executing someone from a rival tribe or political faction. A victim's hands and feet are bound, then a tire filled with gasoline is placed around his neck and he is set alight. Even more than the shooting, that phone call was my you're-not-in-Kansas moment. This assignment was going to be like nothing I'd ever done before. This place was like nowhere I'd ever been.

At the time of the incident, Stefanie and the kids were still back in the States. The plan had been for me to precede them by a few weeks to make arrangements for schools and housing and to get my reporting legs under me.

I wasn't able to get to a phone to call her until after I'd had the bullet surgically removed, which happened later in the day. This was not a conversation I relished. "You're not going to believe what happened to me," I began, affecting a breezy tone. To my surprise Stefanie replied, "Yeah, you got shot but you're going to be fine. Great job getting things set up!" In the time between the shooting and the surgery, news of the incident had filtered back to the Post, and the foreign editor had already phoned Stef to let her know that, as he put it, "Paul took a bullet."

Stefanie hopped on a plane the next day. By the time she arrived at the hospital, she was the spouse of a minor celebrity. Mandela had paid me a well-wishers visit the day before. He wanted South Africans and the world to know that his party did not condone violence against journalists. The nurses were star struck. They doted on Stefanie and me. They even gave her a room next to mine in the hospital.

Despite lobbying from Norm and Bea, neither of us gave a moment's thought to abandoning our African adventure. Looking back on it now, these were the most vivid years of our family life. Our kids were all teenagers. Had we stayed in the States, they were at an age when they'd begin drifting away from the nest. But in Africa we were bound together by the drama and danger of the history we were witnessing. Our tight-knit community of journalists and expats was full of flamboyant characters. Parents and their children frequently socialized together. We'd gather for big *bries* (barbecues) on Sunday afternoons, where the reporters who'd dodged bullets during the week would drink a lot of wine and tell a lot of war stories. Most of us lived in the lap of luxury. The Washington Post house had a tennis court, swimming pool, and live-in gardener – par for the course. But we lived in a fortress, also par for the course. Our property was surrounded by high walls and barbed wire. At the top of the stairway to the second-floor bedrooms, we had a floor-to-ceiling iron gate that could be secured with a padlock. This was the "rape gate," designed to keep intruders from doing their worst. Nope, not Kansas.

During our three-year stay in South Africa, Stef had her own dicey moments, but was tough as nails. With piercing screams and thrashing arms, she fended off a would-be attacker while on a jog in Cape Town. She kept her cool when a pedestrian with an AK-47 approached the car menacingly while she was stopped at a red light in Joburg on her morning commute taking the three kids to school. When our car broke down on a highway adjacent to Khayelitsha, one of the country's most violent townships, she and Jeremy, our oldest, calmly hitched a ride to the nearby Cape Town airport, where she floored the folks at the car rental counter when she told them where she'd left me and the two younger kids in our broken-down car. This was long before there were cell-phones to keep everyone in touch with everyone, 24/7. Eventually, Stef and Jeremy and a tow-truck came to our rescue, without incident.

Stef's favorite not-in-Kansas story is about her first excursion to the supermarket near our home in the fancy northern suburbs of Joburg. "There's a walk-through metal detector. When I go through it, it starts beeping. I'm not sure what to do, so I keep walking. Then I hear the uniformed guard say something. At first, I can't make it out; I'm still getting used to the accent. Then I piece it together. He's told me: 'It's okay. It must just be madam's gun.'"

A few weeks after my shooting, the cops arrested four teenagers they had picked up in my stolen rental car. This was remarkable. In South Africa back then (and still now), carjacking was something of a national pastime. Cases almost never got solved. It was widely assumed that the criminal gangs that run the carjacking rings were protected by dirty cops. Plus, the cops back then had no love for the likes of Phillip and me. But our shooting had been big news all over South Africa, so they were under pressure to show that, amidst the low-grade anarchy, they could still impose a modicum of law and order.

Shortly after the arrest, Phillip and I were summoned to a police station to identify the suspects in a lineup. Everyone who's ever watched a cop show knows what that scene looks like. But this one wasn't anything like that. Our lineup consisted of roughly two dozen men of various sizes and ages assembled in the station courtyard. Going in, Phillip and I had been worried that the police might be railroading the teenage suspects. We were conflicted. Yes, we wanted justice; no, we didn't want to be accomplices to police misconduct. We agreed we wouldn't make a positive identification unless we were absolutely sure of it.

I was the first to be taken into the courtyard. I gave the sprawling lineup a long hard look. I had absolutely no flash of recognition of any kind. Zip. Nada. I was still a newcomer in South Africa; I didn't have my bearings about much of anything. As I was being escorted out, I was cursing myself under my breath. "You fucked up. And what happens when Phillip does make an identification? What a mess."

That turned out not to be a problem. Phillip also came away empty. The trial proceeded anyway. The two of us were sitting next to each other in the courtroom when the four young defendants were marched in. In an instant, we looked at each other with the same thought: "Yup, that's them."

Hard to imagine a more powerful object lesson in the frailty of human observation. In one setting, you see one thing. Change the setting, you're still looking at the same thing, but you see it differently. Until that point of my life as a reporter, I'd put a lot of stock in eyewitness accounts. From then on, not as much.

Phillip and I were both called to the stand to testify. We each described the incident. At the key point of our cross-examinations, we were each asked whether we had been able to identify the suspects at that police station lineup. We each said we couldn't. The charges of carjacking and attempted murder were dropped. The four defendants were convicted of receiving stolen goods.

Phillip and I have stayed in touch over the years. After spending a chunk of time in the U.S. and Europe, he's back in South Africa, doing investigative journalism. We both know we've spent the second half of our lives on bonus time. Our shared wisdom about our near-death experience amounts to nothing more profound than this: life sometimes turns on dumb luck. Or in our cases, inches and centimeters. We both doubt that the last three decades have been as kind to our young assailants as they've been to us. Neither of us has regrets about the way the trial played out, though I do recall something Phillip said as we left the courtroom: "I wish I'd gone over to the kid who shot me and told him: 'Asshole, at least give me back my wallet.'"

~

"There are lots of ways to die in Africa." That's what veteran foreign correspondent Remer Tyson told me when we met a month or so after I arrived. Even after my shocking introduction, I thought he was laying it on thick. Nope. During my three years in South Africa, six journalists lost their lives. Two were members of the Bang-Bang

Club,[19] nickname for a group of South African photographers who spent their lives racing from hot spot to hot spot, fueled by adrenalin. You throw yourself into the middle of enough firefights, a bullet may find you. Ken Oosterbroek was killed while filming a crossfire between black township militia and South African defense forces. Not long afterwards, his best friend Kevin Carter committed suicide – distraught not just over Ken's death but over the controversy stirred up by a Pulitzer-prize winning photo he had taken of a vulture hovering near a naked, starving child in famine-ridden, war-torn Sudan. Critics wondered why he hadn't intervened to help the child. In fact he did, right after he took the photo. Not long after Kevin returned from a bittersweet trip to New York where he was feted for his Pulitzer but also had to fend off critics of his prize-winning photo, he and I bumped into each other in Mozambique while we were covering the civil war there. We didn't know each other well, but he poured his heart out to me over a boozy dinner one night in Maputo. Two weeks later he killed himself. I had no idea.

I had several other close calls. A month after the carjacking, my arm still in a sling, I joined a dozen or so other foreign correspondents to cover a huge protest march called by Mandela's party against the government of Ciskei, one of the nominally independent black homelands that had been created by the apartheid regime. As tens of thousands of protesters approached the capital buildings in Bisho, hidden Ciskei defense forces opened fire with automatic weapons. I was in the front lines of the march, not far from Cyril Ramaphosa, South Africa's current president. The shots seemed to come from the front of us, from the left of us; from the right of us. At first, I thought they were warning shots. Then I realized that people around me had

---

[19]   *Another club member, my friend Joao Silva, nearly died in 2010 when he stepped on a landmine in Afghanistan. Eighty operations and two prosthetic legs later, he's back to being a superb photojournalist. He also runs marathons on a hand-cranked bike and tools around South Africa on a souped-up motorcycle.*

been hit. We had marched into an ambush. There was no escape. A few yards away, marchers threw their bodies over Ramaphosa and other protest leaders, shielding them. The barrage lasted for several minutes – all of it carried live on South Africa television and radio, which Stefanie was listening to to while driving to pick up the kids from school. Twenty-eight marchers were killed in the massacre, more than 200 wounded. Thousands of rounds of bullets had been fired. None found me. Dumb luck.

A year and a half later I covered another infamous shootout in another black homeland – Bophuthatswana. It was a month before the historic election that would bring Mandela to power. This was a terrifying prospect for South Africa's right-wing extremists. Most were Afrikaners – the white tribe of Africa. It was their people who had created apartheid and enforced it with ruthless brutality. With the oppressed majority about to take over, they feared a retribution that would be equally vicious. Unlike the whites who traced their roots to England, Afrikaners had no place to go. This had been their only home for the three centuries since their Dutch ancestors had put down stakes in the southernmost tip of the continent. Several thousand of them – mostly farmers with their pickup trucks, their rifles, their bullets and their booze – had converged on Bop from all over South Africa to make a last stand. They were under the illusion that by joining up with the defense forces of the apartheid-friendly black puppet regime in Bop, they could somehow keep the election – and the future – from happening. Back then I compared them in print to the Ku Klux Klan. A more apt analogy today would be the Proud Boys on January 6.

When my great friend John Battersby and I arrived in the capital city of Mmabatho, the scene was pure chaos. Rather than being embraced as fellow defenders of the status quo, the white militiamen were under attack by the allies they thought they had in the Bop defense forces. There were shoot-outs all over the place. No one was in control of the streets. No one knew where to go, what to do, who was on whose side.

John and I got wind that many of the Afrikaners were holed up at a Bop military base they had commandeered on the outskirts of town. We drove out to take a look. Bad idea. They'd been licking their wounds, drinking prodigiously, contemplating the end of the world as they knew it. Wrong place, wrong time to ask them questions. After we identified ourselves, the thugs at the gate pummeled our car with their rifle butts and roughed us up. I got away with a black eye, fat lip and bloody nose; John had a patch of hair pulled from the top of his head. Coulda been worse. Dumb luck.

My scariest moment in Africa came while I was covering the civil war in Angola. This time my reporting companion was Willi Germund, a correspondent for a chain of German newspapers. While we were making the rounds in the capital city of Luanda, we each picked up reports that the rebels had just committed atrocities in a village near Benguela, about 250 miles to the south. Our job is to bear witness, so we hit the road. What we didn't know, and what the local sources we relied on for intel also didn't know, is that the day or days before, rebels had overtaken and now controlled parts of the main coastal roadway.

A couple of hours into the drive, I was dozing in the passenger seat when the rat-tat-tat of bullets woke me. I looked out the car window to see a couple of rebel soldiers with the AK-47s they had just fired. I looked over at Willi, assuming he would gun the accelerator. Instead he hit the brakes.

That turned out to be the right call. We had driven into a rebel checkpoint. A few hundred feet down the highway lay the mangled remains of a bridge they must have just blown up. Had we tried to outrun our problem, we wouldn't have gotten far. We might have gotten killed.

Our captors looked to be no more than 16 or 17 years old. We showed them our press cards. It wasn't clear if this meant anything to them. None of us spoke a common language. One of them cranked up his walkie- talkie, presumably to get instructions about what to do with us. Between his broken Portuguese and our broken Spanish, he let us know we were going to be taken by foot to a nearby rebel base camp.

Off we went into the African bush. After maybe ten minutes, we came to a clearing. There was no sign of a rebel camp. This was just an open space in the middle of the jungle. In the middle of nowhere. On the far side of the earth. Hmm, I thought, this is where I'm going to die. In my other misadventures, events had moved too fast for me to register fear. This time, I was pretty certain I was going to be killed. I mulled over my options. Run? Try to overpower our captors? These were not viable options. They had automatic weapons and the seasoned judgment of teenagers. I looked over at Willi, who seemed as helpless and frightened as I was. I thought about Stefanie. I thought about our kids – how sad it was that I wouldn't get a chance to see them grow up. I was in a silent panic. I didn't know what to think, except that the end was near.

But it wasn't. After a few excruciating minutes, another pair of rebels arrived. Turns out the clearing was a transfer point. Our new captors proceeded to march us another half mile or so to the rebel camp.

Where we were treated quite well! The commander was intrigued to have a couple of Western journalists in his camp. He was especially pleased to host a Washington Post reporter. His movement was led by Jonas Savimbi, a ruthless and charismatic figure who was a darling of American conservatives and a longtime beneficiary of covert support from the CIA, which valued him as a bulwark against the spread of communism in Africa. "Tell me," the commander asked after we had made our introductions, "what do the Americans really think about our war?" I didn't have the heart to tell him that the vast majority of Americans had no fucking clue there was a war. I said they hoped for peace.

During our first day of captivity, he was vague about what would happen to us. Even rebel movements have bureaucracies; clearly, he was awaiting instructions, probably from Savimbi himself. This could mean trouble. Savimbi, having broken his word and backed out of too many hard-won peace agreements, had fallen out of favor with his superpower backer.

So we settled in for the night. The food was foul but the guerillas were friendly. We hoped that by the next morning we would get some word about our fate. No such luck. Willi speculated that they were planning to take us to the rebel headquarters in the interior of the country, hundreds of miles away, perhaps to use us as a bargaining chip for who knows what. We both began to wrap our minds around the idea that we were in for a long haul. Willi was a bit of an adrenalin junkie; he seemed innervated. I was appalled.

To pass the time, we tore paper from our reporter's notepads into shreds and made them into chess pieces. Willi and I split the first two games. As we were about to start the third, the commander appeared in our hut and flashed our car keys. He motioned for us to look outside, where we saw our rented Mercedes, bearing bullet holes from the encounter we'd had at the checkpoint.

"You can go back to Luanda," he told us. We shook his hand and drove north. Dumb luck.

~

I look back now at those years in Africa with the same incredulity I felt at the time. Did all that shit really happen to me?? Just to weave it all together into one narrative – as I'm doing now for the first time – feels almost like an out-of-body experience.

Back then, it also triggered another set of feelings. I felt sorta like Superman. I'd stared death in the face, kept my cool, survived. Not bad! I even started having dreams that featured me flying. No I wasn't a caped crusader saving the world. But I was able to float through the air, free as a bird, leaving people on the ground astonished by my superpower. Great dreams! Used to have them all the time. Miss them.

Filing stories from Africa was always an adventure. Decades later I'm having nightmares about the IT challenges.

Have you read any of the books about the sling-shot effect that World War II had on the GIs who survived it? They came back home brimming with self-confidence and civic energy. They used it to build everything from interstate highways to middle-class suburbs to space-ships that reached for the moon to global institutions that under-girded a rules-based, American-led international order. They were dubbed the Greatest Generation. They thought they could do any-thing. Long story short, they were more right than wrong.

That was me when I came back from Africa in 1995. And it led to the next time I made news – when I left journalism.

My editors at the Post wanted me to go back to covering presi-dential campaigns, which is where I'd spent most of my career before taking the detour to Africa. I had misgivings. I'd been attracted to the campaign beat because I'd been raised on the Kennedy/Camelot myth that politics was the arena where great men fought glorious battles over big ideas to win the public's mandate to make wise policy. What a show! What a thrill to have a front-row seat.

Covering four presidential campaigns stripped me of my inno-cence. After the 1988 campaign, I wrote a book about how dreary and dysfunctional political campaigns had become – not the feast of democracy I'd imagined, but the junk food. I took swipes at all the key actors – the candidates, the voters, the political consultants, the media. The biggest problem, as I saw it, was that the campaign dialogue was held almost entirely in attack ads and sound bites. We were in an era when cable television was in its infancy, MSNBC and Fox News did not yet exist, nor did the internet and social media. The three broadcast networks – CBS, NBC, and ABC – enjoyed an effective monopoly on campaign coverage. If it didn't happen on the big three, it didn't happen. But instead of providing substantive cov-erage of serious issues, the broadcast networks treated political cam-paigns as a chance to make a buck. Come election season, candidates spent most of their waking hours dialing for dollars, going deeper into hock to special interests – all so they could buy their way onto the air, 30 seconds at a time. In a cynical age, the most effective ads were deceptive attacks designed to keep the other guy's supporters from showing up on Election Day. Voter turnout in that 1988 campaign fell to its lowest level in a century. Somebody needed to do something! The last chapter of my book proposed that Congress pass a law requiring that, in return for their free use of the public's airwaves, the broadcasters air short nightly segments during the closing weeks of the campaign in which the candidates could talk about their policy proposals. I thought it was a great idea. The powers that be didn't. Not the broadcasters, who profited mightily from the sale of air time for political ads. Not members of Congress, who opposed any reform that leveled the playing field for challengers. The book *See How They Run: Electing the President in the Age of Mediaocracy* didn't sell very well. My idea went nowhere. Okay, I told myself, if that's how it is, I'm off to Africa.

Nelson Mandela's 1994 inauguration as president of South Africa attracted more than a hundred heads of state, many from Third World countries. Other than Mandela himself, the most popular man at the VIP luncheon was Fidel Castro. When I asked him to explain why, he hesitated for a moment to inspect the press badge dangling from my neck, which identified me a Washington Post reporter. Then he smiled. "I owe it all to your country," he said.

Now I'm back, feeling like Superman. And also feeling less jaded about politics. I'd just covered one of the most inspiring political campaigns in human history. The candidate of the oppressed had defeated the candidate of the oppressors. There was violence but no race war. Against all odds, the center held. This was a negotiated revolution, piloted by a pair of canny and courageous adversaries – Mandela and F.W. deKlerk, co-winners of the Nobel Peace Prize (even though they barely could stand to be in the same room with one another). Once in office, Mandela pursued reconciliation rather than vengeance. Remarkable! And I came home thinking: By God, if they can get politics right in South Africa, I bet we can get it right in America.

So I dusted off my old idea, put on my cape and came flying to the rescue.

My first piece of business was to quit my job. This left my editors gob-smacked. In the Post newsroom back then (and still now), the greatest sin a reporter could commit was to defect to the New York Times. But leaving journalism altogether at the height of your career to become a goo-goo reformer was beyond sin. It was flat out bonkers. My bosses were all friends of mine. One by one, they tried to bring me to my senses. But I was a man on a mission.

At the end of my last day at the Post, after a series of awkward goodbyes, I went upstairs to visit the legendary Ben Bradlee. Ben was no longer running the newsroom; he had a sinecure two floors above, where he was vice president in charge of being Ben Bradlee. By the time I made my way up to his office, I was a bit shell-shocked. As I told him about my big idea, I was girding for yet another tongue-lashing. To my surprise, he listened patiently, paternally. It probably helped that we were tennis buddies. And that he was no longer in the trenches on the fifth floor. In any case, he did something unexpected. He asked: "How can I help?"

"Umm, well, do you know Walter Cronkite?"

"Of course I know Walter!" At which point Ben rolled up his right pant leg and tapped on his knee. "Hear that? Titanium. I just had it put in two months ago. Walter got his last month. We're on the phone with each other all the time talking about our new knees."

"Well listen, I've read that Cronkite is as pissed off at the broadcasters as I am. If I could recruit him to the cause, this thing could really take off."

"I'll give him a call."

Much as I appreciated the offer, I sorta figured that "I'll give him a call" was a pleasantry on the order of "Let's have lunch." But, hey, better than another lecture.

Like Ben, Stef was there for me. At the time, two of our children were in college and the third was not far behind. We had big tuition bills and almost no savings. I'd just quit the Post without knowing where my next paycheck would come from. When we broke the news to the kids, one of them asked Stef, "How much money do you make from selling your jewelry?" She delivered the bad news with her usual relish. "Not quite enough to pay for your textbooks." In retrospect, I'm astounded at how reckless I was. I'm also amazed by Stef's forbearance. But not surprised. She knew this was something I felt I had to do. She told the children that everything was going to work out okay. And she assured me that, no, I wasn't off my rocker. I suspect she had her doubts.

When I got home the evening after my chat with Ben, the telephone rang. "Hello Paul," said the Voice of God. "This is Walter Cronkite. Ben tells me you have an interesting idea."

Readers my age don't need a primer to know what a journalistic and cultural icon Cronkite was. But for you young ones out there, he was like…he was like…well, that's the point. There's no one anymore like Walter Cronkite. These days the media ecosystem is as polarized as the country it reports on. It has no authority figures. Back in Cronkite's heyday, when he was anchoring the CBS Evening News in the turbulent 1960s and 1970s, he was "the most trusted man in America," a claim backed by public opinion surveys. When he closed his newscast every night with his reassuring signature line: "And that's the way it is," America believed him. Imagine that – a world where we all agree on the facts.

When he made that phone call to me, Cronkite like Bradlee was mostly in retirement. His successor as CBS news anchor, Dan Rather, didn't relish the idea of working in his shadow. So Cronkite was confined to doing occasional special reports about the space program and other favorite topics. But within the broadcast industry itself, he still packed a punch. He served on the board of CBS's parent corporation, where he was a sharp internal critic, especially of its failure to do a better job covering political campaigns. Walter, like me, thought the broadcasters should be required to provide free air time to the candidates. They had been granted licenses valued at tens of billions of dollars, free of charge, to operate the public's airwaves. In return they had pledged to serve the public interest. Instead, they were profiteering on the most important thing we do in a democracy.

It didn't take a genius to figure out that with Cronkite on board, I could attract pretty much anyone I wanted to the cause. In a matter of weeks, I lined up foundation funding. Not long after that, I recruited former Presidents Jimmy Carter and Gerald Ford to join Cronkite as the honorary co-chairs of the new reform group I created, The Free TV for Straight Talk Coalition. The organization consisted of the three of them, my telephone, my fax machine and me. Our office was in one of the spare bedrooms in our mostly empty nest house.

But boy we took off! In the blink of an eye, our reform movement became big news in all the top newspapers and news magazines. It was the lead Talk of the Town article in The New Yorker; if there's such a thing as ground zero for high-end journalism, that's it. Cronkite and two ex-presidents obviously brought gravitas to our crusade, but the focus of most of the coverage turned out, surprisingly, to be on me. The same newsroom DNA that had left my editors dumbfounded at my mid-career leap led others to see me as a great man-bites-dog story. I became "The Man on a Mission"; "The Crusader Who Made TV Blink"; "The Screen Saviour."[20] There were less flattering headlines too: "Tilting at Windmills"; "Quixotic" etc. But when you're on a mission to save the world, there ain't no such thing as bad publicity. In short order, I parlayed the press attention into additional foundation funding, along with support from more politicians and partnerships with campaign reform groups all over the country.

For a while, we were rocking. We ran full page ads in the Times and Post in which Cronkite, Carter and Ford used their elder statesmen halos to bash the broadcasters for failing to step up to their public service obligations. This got the broadcasters' attention. In the 1996 campaign, they voluntarily provided a small number of free air time segments – enough, they hoped, to get us off their backs and the issue off the front pages. We wanted much more. For the next several years we pushed for systemic reform, either through legislation or regulation. The chairman of the Federal Communications Commission at the time was Reed Hundt. He and I knew each other from our days at college, where in successive years, we'd each served as executive editor of the Yale Daily News. Reed was a big supporter of free air time. So were his political patrons, President Clinton and

------

[20]   *Not long after we launched, I gave a presentation about free air time to a meeting of civic activists in Chicago. At the end of the talk, a skinny black guy with a funny name and big ears came up to the podium and introduced himself. He said he'd just been elected to the state senate and told me I had a great idea. That's how I met Barack Obama.*

Vice President Gore. And so was Sen. John McCain,[21] the great champion of campaign finance reform.

McCain, Cronkite and me jawboning broadcasters.

---

[21]   *Working with McCain was a hoot. He hated phonies and sacred cows. And he had a mouth. He used to say of a several of senate colleagues: "Dumber than a flat tire." I recall a lunch we had at a fancy restaurant in Chicago with Bob Iger, chairman of ABC. Our mission was to persuade him to provide free candidate air time on his TV stations. I opened the pitch. McCain, unimpressed, cut me off. "Bob, let me tell you something. Taylor here is a nice guy. But I'm not a nice guy. You don't want to be on the wrong side of this." At the time, McCain was chairman of the powerful Senate Commerce Committee. He didn't make a specific threat. He didn't need to. Iger understood McCain could make life difficult for any industry he put in his cross hairs. I remember thinking at the time: So this is how reform happens! But I was mistaken. Iger came through with a bit of window dressing. We wanted systemic change. Never got there.*

Me evangelizing.

Lots of firepower. But never quite enough. The status quo is very good at preserving the status quo. McCain did get a campaign finance bill through Congress, but broadcast industry lobbyists had little trouble stripping away its free air time provision before the bill came to a final vote. Clinton spent the final years of his second term weakened by the Monica Lewinsky scandal and subsequent impeachment proceedings. He had no appetite for pushing a reform that was unpopular with members of Congress on both sides of the aisle. With the White House distracted and disengaged, any hope for a regulatory breakthrough via the FCC was also gone.

The early 2000s brought a change in the media ecosystem that put the final stake in my free air time campaign. Cable news surged onto the market and opened up a huge new platform for campaign coverage on television. One reason that the traditional broadcasters had steered away from political speech is that they feared it would send their viewers scrambling for the remote. CNN, Fox and MSNBC, by contrast, embraced it as ratings gold. Their niche audiences were made up of news junkies and political partisans. Suddenly there was a gusher of debates, interviews, punditry and campaign coverage all over cable. As we've come to discover, this has led to an entirely different kind of political dystopia. But whatever else it did, cable news cut the legs out from under my case for free air time. After nearly eight years, I let go of my baby and moved on to the Pew Research Center. At the time I consoled myself that I'd had a great idea whose time never came. Looking back now, through the lens of our animated but often rancid culture of political discourse on television, it doesn't seem like such a great idea after all. More on that later.

For now, let's turn to my least comfortable 15 minutes of fame. And let's start with the opening paragraph of that Talk of the Town article in The New Yorker, which posited that I'd left journalism because I couldn't come to terms with the role I'd played in the demise of Gary Hart's presidential candidacy.

"When it comes to living down marital notoriety, Hester Prynne has nothing on the Washington Post reporter Paul Taylor. Ever since the 1988 Presidential race, Taylor has been symbolically tattooed with a giant "A" for having the audacity to ask Gary Hart if he ever committed adultery. For better or worse, what came to be called the Big A Question forever changed the rules on public discussion of private philandering. The question also changed history, leading inexorably to Hart's withdrawal from the Presidential race and prompting a huge and wildly divided outpouring of views. Betty Friedan exulted, perhaps overconfidently, "This is the last time a candidate will be able to treat women as bimbos," while one Hart supporter excoriated Taylor for making Hart "the first American victim of Islamic justice – he has been politically stoned to death for adultery.

"Taylor argued… that neither he nor the Post could be faulted for having asked Hart "the question he asked for."

I'm guessing most older readers remember something about the Hart scandal, at least in broad strokes. A recap: In the spring of 1987, shortly after Hart had launched his front-running campaign for the Democratic presidential nomination, the Miami Herald, acting on a tip and its own eyewitness surveillance, reported that he had just spent the night at his Washington DC townhouse with a woman who – as follow-up reporting would quickly reveal – was a Miami model half his age and not his wife. Hart denied everything, insisted he always held himself to the highest standards of morality, and attacked the press for getting the story wrong and for coarsening the public square with lurid journalism. Two days later, when he faced the press for the first time, I asked him if he considered adultery to be immoral. He said he did. I then asked if he had ever committed adultery. He said that wasn't a fair question and declined to answer it.

In those intervening two days the Post newsroom had been inundated with tips about other alleged Hart affairs. This was hardly a surprise. Hart had a reputation as a brazen philanderer. But it also presented us with a dilemma. The longstanding newsroom rule about such matters was that private behavior goes unreported unless it impacts public behavior. Should we stick with that rule? Or, in the wake of the Herald story and Hart's indignant denial, break it?

I was the Post reporter on the campaign trail covering Hart. I was offended by his behavior, his deceit and most of all his attempt to shield himself in a cloak of moral superiority. I knew my editors were still trying to figure out what to do with those other tips. But I decided to take matters in my own hands. At the press conference, I pounced.

This was unlike me. I'd never been a "gotcha" reporter. But this struck me as a no-brainer, especially since a few weeks earlier, an exasperated Hart, frustrated with stories that regurgitated rumors about his "zipper problem," had challenged reporters to "follow me around. I don't care. I'm serious. If anyone wants to put a tail on me, go ahead. They'd be very bored."

As I saw it, all I did was ask Hart the question he'd invited and circumstances demanded. Not everyone agreed. Overnight, the "Big A Question" became a topic of zealous debate among journalists, politicians and the public at large. Was adultery now something the campaign press should be policing on a regular basis? Were adulterers now disqualified for elective office? To me, the easy answers were: no and no. But if you're stupid enough to get yourself into the sort of pickle that Hart had gotten himself into, don't expect the press to look the other way.

A few hours after that press conference, Gary Hart dropped out of the race. A few days after that, the National Enquirer ran a photo of Hart with the Miami woman, Donna Rice. It had been taken the month before, when the two of them were on an overnight cruise to Bimini on a charter boat haplessly named The Monkey Business. She was sitting on his lap. Both were wearing naughty smiles and silly T-shirts. It didn't look like they'd been trying to figure out how to balance the federal budget. Hart was 50 years old. A political career rich in promise and possibility was over in a flash. Whatever else this was, it was a profound tragedy for him.

As for me, I had defenders and critics. But most of all, I had my Scarlet Letter. I became the guy who asked the fatal question. Did I do right? Did I do wrong? You can decide for yourself. Looking back now, here's my take: Politicians are entitled to a zone of privacy, and their sex lives fall within in. We should never traffic in unconfirmed rumors about zipper problems. However, if they behave without discretion, all bets are off. In this formulation, being recklessly promiscuous is different from being quietly adulterous. If that's a standard which winks at discreet hypocrisies, so be it. Hypocrisy is the homage vice pays to virtue. And to social comity. [22]

I wrote those last few sentences in my 1990 book; I wouldn't change a word today. So no, I wouldn't have done anything differently. But I wish events had played out differently. I have more empathy for Hart now than I did in the moment. I'm perplexed that he never found his way past the scandal. Much has changed in the Me-Too era, but even now, the public tends to be forgiving about sexual indiscretions in high places – otherwise Bill Clinton and Donald Trump would never have made it to the White House. Unless the behavior is predatory, sex scandals typically follow a similar arc – after the blow-up, the storm passes and a forgiving public moves on. Over in London, the hacks of Fleet Street have long had a play book for the phases of coverage of the typical British sex scandal: exposed, enjoyed, ignored.

This year's release of the Epstein files has been an exception that proves the rule. Prominent men on both sides of the Atlantic have had their reputations destroyed by relentless media coverage. In the

------

[22] *Four decades later, that murky newsroom standard prevails. Yes we've had sex scandals in high places, but for every Jennifer Flowers, Monica Lewinsky and Stormy Daniels, there are countless paramours whose names and stories never surface, because the adulterers are discreet.*

pecking order of scandal, the sex trafficking of underage girls makes an adulterous fling with a consenting adult seem almost quaint by comparison. I wish Hart had found a way to show contrition, ask for forgiveness, and fight his way back to public life. I've never understood why he didn't.

For my part, I wish I'd never been saddled with that scarlet letter. The New Yorker piece speculated that it threw me into a midlife crisis that triggered my departure from journalism. Yes and no. It surely contributed to my decision to stop covering political campaigns. But leaving journalism was a different proposition altogether. I thought then – I still think now – that journalism is a noble calling. It matters because reality matters. Reporters do vital work. We give readers and viewers the information they need to make their lives, societies and governments better. We shine light on dark places and tell truth to power. We write the first rough draft of history.[23] The work is hard and can be dangerous. We sometimes get things wrong. Given the pressure of deadlines and the fog of reality, how could we not? But we keep hacking away. Didn't find the whole truth today? Ok, maybe tomorrow.

In light of this lifelong love affair with journalism, why did I leave? One way to explain it is that I knew I was good but I also knew I wasn't good enough. I had the talent and drive to become a national political reporter for the Washington Post, where I was part of a superb staff led by my professional north star, David Broder. But having made it to the top, I looked around and saw other political reporters at the Post and elsewhere who were better, faster, smarter, more committed. I had a ball covering the big show, but I had my limits. I didn't want to spend those extra days out on the road, getting to know this up-and-coming congressman or that longtime power broker. I'd rather be home with the kids. All of this left me conflicted. I wished my

---

[23]   *That quote is from Phil Graham, the brilliant publisher of the Washington Post who took his own life in 1963, at age 48. He suffered from bipolar disorder.*

stories were better. I wished they were easier to write. I wished the demands of the job weren't so steep. I was frustrated with my career, disappointed with myself.

I poured some of those frustrations into that book about how anemic campaigns had become. After it was published, I asked my editors if I could step away from political coverage and create a new beat about children, families, poverty and public policy. I argued that these topics deserved more attention than the Post had been giving them. Warily, they agreed. I wrote some decent stories, nothing ground-breaking. When the South Africa bureau opened up, I leapt. I was primed for a new adventure. Lucky me, Stefanie and our three teenage kids were willing to uproot their lives and come along for the ride.

Africa turned out to be the family adventure of a lifetime. In the decades since, whenever we're all together, we'll often revel, marvel and delight in our memories – our magnificent Rhodesian Ridgeback Brutus; our gentle gardener Bernard; their multi-cultural, multi-racial school, Redhill, with its thatched roofs, stiff-upper-lip British headmaster and take-no-prisoners ex-special forces rugby coach. All that, plus all those close calls!

I got more than I bargained for on the danger front, but it led to an unexpected discovery: I'm a cool customer under duress. This wasn't a test I'd set out to take, but it's one I was pleased to have passed. As for my work product, when I left that continent after three years, I was able to say to myself: You know what, you did just fine. It was a complicated story. You got the big picture right. You wrote some pretty good pieces, especially for someone who never really knew the territory. And you got the chance to bear witness to history. I was at peace at last with my career as a hack. And so I gave myself permission to leave my day job as a newspaper reporter.

In the decades since, I've written scores of free-lance articles for multiple publications on a range of topics. My favorite – probably because it, too, broke the rule about reporters not being a part of their stories – ran on The Post's op-ed page the day Mandela died at the age of 95.

Mandela Knew How to Deploy
the Moral High Ground

December 5, 2013

When, after 27 years, Nelson Mandela was finally released from prison, the world marveled at his generous spirit, even temperament, genteel manners, disarming wit, ready smile and lack of bitterness.

Admirable as they were, those saintly virtues don't begin to explain his political genius. Mandela was also cunning, iron-willed, bull-headed, contemptuous — and more embittered than he let on. He needed all of his traits — soft and hard — to engineer a political miracle: persuading a sitting government to negotiate its own abdication by yielding power to the very people it had ruthlessly oppressed.

Historic transfers of that magnitude typically occur only at gunpoint. To pull it off peacefully, Mandela knew that he had to tame the racial fears and hatreds that have haunted beautiful South Africa since the first whites settled there four centuries ago. He needed to teach militant blacks that they couldn't take revenge and frightened whites that they shouldn't fear retribution.

Mandela didn't do all that by himself. On both sides of the racial divide, he had the help of legions of sophisticated negotiators determined to find a peaceful path to democracy. His main partner, President Frederik W. de Klerk, was a shrewd Afrikaner who had the foresight to understand that the grotesque apartheid system he once championed was destroying his country, and he had the fortitude to stick with his surrender-without-a-fight strategy through four arduous years of start-and-stop negotiations, even as the deal grew less attractive for the white minority that had put him in power.

The two men never got on well. And Mandela had no compunctions about using de Klerk as a scapegoat whenever it served his purposes. At a news conference in Oslo, Norway the day before they were honored as co-recipients of the 1993 Nobel Peace, Mandela repeated his (dubious) accusation that de Klerk was the mastermind behind deadly faction fighting among rival black groups. The charge infuriated de Klerk but played well among militants in the black townships.

Mandela sometimes used his martyr's halo like a club against his own supporters. At a campaign rally in 1994, when some rowdy black youths ripped down the banner of a small political party they considered corrupt, Mandela called them "hooligans" and "animals" and said they were a disgrace to the liberation movement. He ordered the chastened teenagers to rehang the banner, which they promptly did.

But as the rally was breaking up, he gave them back their dignity. He told them that he loved them and that they would be comrades forever. Scold, flatter, demand, cajole — when you occupy the moral high ground, your tactical options are practically limitless. Mandela's genius was knowing how and when to deploy them all.

In those days, South Africa had plenty of white militants too. The most dangerous moment of Mandela's presidential campaign came when several thousand heavily armed whites left their farms and drove to Bophuthatswana, one of the black homelands set up under apartheid, where they planned to join the forces of the pro-apartheid black puppet government and derail the election.

Instead, their presumed allies turned on them, and the day quickly devolved into a bloody, boozy fiasco. A photograph that captured the last gasp of the white militants – published on front pages around the world – depicted a wounded, khaki-clad white farmer pleading for mercy as a young black homeland soldier hovered over him with a rifle. The soldier executed the farmer on the spot.

Two months later Mandela was elected president. It took a few days to count the ballots, and to pass time he invited small groups of foreign correspondents into a hotel suite where he conducted interviews. During my session, I asked about that young black soldier. The day of the incident, candidate Mandela had condemned the shooting and said that the rule of law must prevail. Now that he was about to become president, I asked, would he bring that soldier to justice?

Mandela gave me a cold stare. "Why is it that the Western press would focus so much on that one case when so many thousands of blacks have been the victims of so much political violence for so many years?" I had a response, but my tongue went numb. None of the other reporters in the room dared to venture a follow-up. Case closed. The great man knew how to play the race card.

When our interview session came to a close, I broke one of the cardinal rules of journalism. I handed Nelson Mandela a campaign poster that I had collected as a keepsake and asked him to sign it. He gave me a firm handshake and warm smile and wrote a lovely note. It hangs in my office, where I look at it every day.

Covering Mandela's presidential campaign was the thrill of my life as a hack. The photo directly above was taken a few minutes after he scolded me for asking a question he didn't like.

CHAPTER EIGHT

MAN PLANS, GOD LAUGHS

"Everyone has a plan," heavyweight champ Mike Tyson once philosophized, "until they get punched in the mouth." Generals have said pretty much the same thing about war ever since the first rock was hurled in anger. "No plan survives first contact with the enemy." Based on personal experience I'd put home renovation in the same category. Memoirs too.

About a nano-second after we hatched our plan to renovate the house and write about the renovation, Covid-19 showed up. The prospect of writing my memoir was instantly rendered absurd. I'm going to whine about my troubles when millions of people all over the world are dropping dead in a pandemic? To quote another sports legend, John McEnroe: "You cannot be serious!"

I abandoned the book idea (temporarily, it turned out). But the renovation went forward. We had a head of steam, we needed the distraction, and we had time on our hands. In the five years since I'd left my job at Pew,[24] I'd kept myself busy giving speeches about demographic and generational change to audiences across the country and world. Then along came the pandemic; all those meetings and conventions where I used to present my data were cancelled. The timing was fine by me. I enjoyed the work and had gotten pretty good at leavening my Pew numbers with jokes, anecdotes and commentary, but after you've done your dog-and-pony show a couple of hundred times, you get tired of listening to yourself. It was time to move on.

So off we went.

Since I was no longer planning to write a book, I didn't keep a diary during those construction years. A windfall for you, dear reader. My son-in-law James had a nice description of the yin and yang of our work: "A hundred problems, a hundred solutions…" We never added it to the mantra, but there was a phrase that belonged at the back end to that sentence: "…and a whole lot of drudgery." With no notes to back me up, I'll spare you the drudgery. But I can amuse you with the problems. You have my blessing to join God in a good laugh.

We start with the fact that I neglected to get a building permit. Actually, this was not an oversight. It was a calculated risk that backfired. OK, it was rank stupidity. My thinking was: (A). We're in the middle of a pandemic. None of the county offices are open. There's no one to call. The website is impossible. (B). Our house is well off the main road. The only people who'll know we're doing this are our neighbors, all of whom are relatives or lifelong friends. We're not going to get ratted out. (C). Applying for a building permit would mean getting architectural plans more detailed than the rudimentary drawings we had. We'd already severed our relationship with our architect.

---

[24]   *Not entirely of my own volition. When Pew Research Center founder and president Andrew Kohut stepped down for health reasons, I sought his job but was not chosen for it. The center's parent organization and funder, the Pew Charitable Trusts, wanted more control over the center's operations than Andy and I were comfortable yielding. They brought in an outsider to run in. I was EVP at the time. We worked out an amicable separation.*

There was acrimony. Going back to him would be awkward. (D). This wasn't my first rodeo. I'd neglected to get permits on a few previous DIY projects. I got nailed once. The other times, no problemo.

For the first few weeks, everything zipped along. James and I and a local carpenter named Jesus (I kid you not, though pronounced Hay-Zeus and nicknamed Jessie)) had taken down the old rotted out deck, then sunk the concrete piers and built the columns and joists for a new deck. We had demolished the exterior walls of the kitchen and living room and were about to start building the new dining room inside the "L" that connected those two rooms. Things were going great. Building permits were the last thing on my mind.

So when a pleasant-looking sixty-ish fellow in a plaid shirt came bounding toward the house late one morning, I greeted him with a friendly hello. I thought he was the electrician we were expecting to give us an estimate for what it would cost to tame the jungle of exposed wires hanging where the kitchen wall used to be.

He turned out to be Tom, a Warren County building inspector. Oops. After I fumbled my way past my confusion about who he was, I pointed out the difficulties of making contact with anyone in his office in the midst of the pandemic. Tom was unimpressed. He seemed like a guy who meant business. I quickly surmised it was time to sue for mercy. "Look, you're right, this is entirely on me."

I explained that I was a do-it-yourself homeowner, working with a couple of guys who actually did know what they were doing. I invited him to come inside for a look. "You're under no obligation to do that," he said. "No, please," I replied. In he came. The first thing he saw was that curtain of exposed wires. He seemed slightly appalled. "We have an electrician on the way," I explained. To change the subject, I directed his attention to the magnificent job we'd done installing a new beam to support the bedroom above the kitchen. I'd been worried that when we removed the kitchen wall – a load-bearing wall – the bedroom might wind up on the kitchen floor. But we'd done everything by the book. First we'd built a temporary stud wall next to the wall we were removing. Then we sistered together two lumber laminate beams that had the strength of steel. Then we supported those beams with a column on one side and a super-sized joist hanger on the other. I sunk 58 (!!) nails into that joist hanger, silently congratulating myself each time my hammer struck its target. Then we removed the temporary wall. Presto!!! The second floor bedroom stayed on the second floor. "We're not skimping on the building codes," I told Tom triumphantly. "If anything, we've overbuilt! My kids and grandkids will be living in this house long after I'm gone. I want it to be rock solid."

Tom smiled as he wrote up the stop work order.

It took three weeks to get the drawings we needed for a permit. Very frustrating. I had no one to blame but myself, which made it sting even more. During the hiatus I brooded about who had tipped off Tom. Was it the guy who had delivered a dumpster a few days before? Hmmm, maybe. Or how about the architect we'd fired? Yup, probably him. He knew we'd have no choice but to go back to him, hat in hand, for the additional drawings. Which is exactly what we did. Whereupon he took his sweet time and charged us a pretty penny. Yup, probably him. Very frustrating.

But that wasn't our only problem during the layoff. News of our work stoppage flashed instantly out to the local raccoon community. *Attention shoppers: The kitchen at 24 Ivy Lane has no exterior wall!* And so as Stefanie and I lay in bed the night after our encounter with Tom, cursing our fate, we heard a ruckus coming from the kitchen. Almost certainly raccoons. But in view of the remote chance that it might have been a bear, we chose not to investigate. We spent the night barricaded in our bedroom, listening to the invaders having their little party.

The morning-after scene was pretty ugly – banana peels, bread and cracker crumbs, half eaten peaches, a wrapper from the licorice that the raccoons had somehow extracted from Stefanie's backpack. As anyone who's ever tangled with them knows, raccoons are clever assholes. Bandit faces, mean stares, nimble paws, impeccable memories.

Before the next nightfall, we whipped together a three-front defense. We stored all our food in the refrigerator or behind a closed bathroom door. We put up a makeshift plywood barrier where the kitchen wall used to be. On the advice of Google, we spread Cayenne pepper over all the kitchen counters. And off to bed we went.

Stefanie was not optimistic. "They're going to fucking figure out how to get into the refrigerator," said she. "No way," said I.

Sometime around midnight we again heard a ruckus in the kitchen. Apparently my plywood wall was not entirely racoon-proof. This was not my first tactical fail with these critters. Over the years they'd pawed their way into any number of outdoor garbage bins I'd built.

"Fuck," said Stefanie. "Shit," said I.

But this time, the morning-after scene brought good news. The refrigerator had not been breached. No food had been consumed. The only evidence of raccoons were the paw tracks in the Cayenne pepper.

I spent an hour beefing up the fortifications on that makeshift wall. And that was that. The raccoons never came back. The crisis was over. Lost the opening battle. Took the punch. Won the war.

～

The pandemic brought some silver linings. Our kids and grandkids spent long stretches of that first year up north with us, podded in our family compound while they worked or studied remotely. It was thrilling to watch the little ones grow up, day by day. A new generation; another cycle. It also meant that James could spend more time working with me on the project. When people asked how we divvied up the labor, I loved pointing out the symmetry: "Fifty years ago I helped build this house with my father-in-law. Now I'm rebuilding it with my son-in-law. And both times, I'm the gopher." (A clever line, but not quite right. By my second go-around, I'd picked up a few skills.)

Another unexpected benefit of the pandemic: It forced me to confront some of my flawed assumptions about human nature. All throughout the renovation, we had lots of interactions with local trades-people – plumbers, electricians, sawmill bosses, stone quarry operators, truckers, excavators, hardware store clerks, building supply salespeople. To a person, they all seemed salt of the earth to me. I enjoyed our banter and small talk. We steered clear of politics because our summer community is a blue speck in a MAGA county (Elise Stefanik is the local congressperson) and we didn't want to wreck the camaraderie. But the pandemic was on top of everyone's mind, and it made all of us yearn for human connections. So we often went there, but carefully. Stef was especially good at sticking to the conversational safe spaces – who'd gotten sick? how bad were the symptoms? whose lives had gotten disrupted? how long will all this last? We were both good at knowing what was off limits – masks, cures, origins, China, Fauci, Trump.

Sometimes we slipped. One such encounter came after, on successive days, first a plumber and then the guy who installed our new kitchen counter explained how the Covid-19 death count had been vastly inflated because hospitals were getting $39,000 in extra Medicare money for every death they attributed to Covid. I assumed this was a fake news factoid they'd picked up on Fox. The first time I heard it, I deflected. If "Thou Shall Not Piss Off the Plumber" isn't the Eleventh Commandment, it should be. But when I heard the same thing again the next day, I decided to take it on. I told the counter-top guy that I'd spent a career trying to make sense out of large data sets. One thing that struck me about Covid was that – despite country-to-country variations – if you compared death rates this year in countries where Covid had struck with the average death rates over the previous five years in these same countries, rates were up everywhere, often substantially. That struck me as pretty solid evidence that the numbers weren't being hyped. One thing countries know how to do is count their dead.

My explanation was long-winded. I wasn't sure if the counter-top guy – who owned his small fabricating business – would stick with it. But he did. He didn't interrupt. He didn't get agitated. He didn't try to rebut. He didn't double down. He listened carefully and seemed to let this new information marinate. "Interesting," he said.[25]

How many conversations have I had – how many have any of you readers had – in the past few years with someone from the other tribe that went that way?[26] This one stands out for me because it's the only one I can recall. Truth is, I simply don't have those conversations. I stay inside my bubble. It's too damn weird over there in the other bubble. Those folks have their feelings, and their feelings don't care about my facts.

I never used to see the world this way. I'd spent most of my life believing that people are more or less rational because it's in their self-interest to be rational. This is the benevolent belief system I inherited from my parents. It was reenforced by my years as a political reporter at the Washington Post, where David Broder used to encourage us to periodically take ourselves off the campaign trail to spend time knocking on doors, asking everyday folks about their lives and their political views.

Here's how that typically went: I'd introduce myself and explain what I was up to. People would size me up through their screen door as if I was crazy. "Sorry, pal, you've come to the wrong house. We don't think much about politics here." I would shift gears. "Okay, can I just ask you a few questions about how things are going in your life and in your community?" What I quickly figured out was that if

---

[25] *He might have been observing his own 11th Commandment: Don't piss off the customer.*

[26] *A 2025 Pew survey found that six-in-ten Americans had stopped talking about politics with someone they know because of something that person said.*

you can get past the initial resistance – guess what, most people will open up. They love talking about themselves, telling you their stories, sharing their opinions. Hell, they're glad you asked!

You do this year after year, in neighborhoods all over the country, and you come away with some home truths. Most Americans are good and decent people. They're not always well informed, but they're long on common sense. As for their political views – here's an assessment that seems to come from another galaxy (in fact it comes from the America of the 1980s and 1990s) – they are nuanced. They see both sides of most issues. They're pragmatists, not dogmatists. On the hot button issues – abortion, immigration, gay rights, etc. – yes, they have strong opinions, but most of the time they're also willing to acknowledge the humanity on the other side.

Those home truths had been under stress since the start of the Trump Era, but for me anyway, it was the pandemic that polished them off for good. If tens of millions of Americans could let their dogmas get in the way of their health, they can't be the rational actors I'd thought they were.

I'd be happy to lay the blame for all this on Trump, but that's too easy. He lit a whole bunch of matches. Why was America such a tinderbox? My list of explanations is pretty standard: Start with galloping demographic, racial and cultural change; mix in the rise of social media echo chambers; the growth of income inequality and the decline of institutional trust; then sprinkle all this with a hate-mongering demagogue who has a feral genius for pushing everyone's buttons. Presto! Dystopia.

Periods of disruptive social change are a recurrent feature of modern life. In the 1850s, British poet Matthew Arnold, struggling to reconcile scientific discoveries with religious verities, wrote about a society "wandering between two worlds – one dead, the other powerless to be born." In the 1930s, imprisoned Italian anti-fascist dissident Antonio Gramsci added an ominous kicker to Arnold's famous passage: "The old world is dying and the new world is struggling to be born. Now is the time of monsters."

Whenever dramatic change comes, it comes too fast for the ins and not fast enough for the outs. This is where America is now: everyone pissed off about something. My guess is that the same storms that blew us into this mess will eventually blow us out of it. One birth and one death at a time, the torch will pass and younger generations will take over. Based on the evidence so far, they're likely to be champions of social justice and defenders of individual liberty. But will they also be repairers of the breach? Will they appeal to the better angels of our nature? Or will they be animated by the same toxic brew of grievance, resentment and animus they witnessed in the public square as they came of age?

I don't have a clue. I no longer trust my insights about the present or past. How can I possibly divine the future? Back when I was a political reporter and then a public opinion survey researcher, friends used to ask me all the time who was going to win the next election. I took great pleasure in telling them. It's swell being a seer! But it's also a mug's game. Given my weakness for overestimating the sunny side, my track record was about as impressive as a coin flip. Maybe not even that good. Even so, for decades I'd serve up my prognostications in lively lectures at our community house in Fourth Lake. As one of my presidential picks after another – Mario Cuomo, Al Gore, Hillary Clinton – somehow never made it to the White House, my credibility kept cratering. "I hope Paul doesn't jinx another one," became the standing joke in the audience. Of all the things one aspires to be in life, a punch line is not among them. Eventually it dawned on me that the future was going to arrive anyway, unbidden by me. I moth-balled my crystal ball.[27]

Long story short, the older I get, the less I think I know. Is this wisdom? Exhaustion? Don't know that either. Strange: you take your long journey only to discover, near the finish line, you never knew where you were going. And that so much of what you thought was true isn't. As 80-year-old brain aneurysm survivor Joni Mitchell put it mournfully when she half-sang, half-spoke her signature lyric at the 2024 Grammy Awards show: "I really don't know life at all." Is this the booby prize for growing old?

That stop work order was the low point of that first year working on the project. The low point of year two was the rupture to my left quad tendon. It happened when I took a rare morning off from the project to hit some tennis balls with an old friend. Out of nowhere, my tendon spontaneously gave out. Or maybe I tripped over my own feet. (Let's agree on version one.) Either way, I went down in a heap. The jolt of pain was identical to what I'd felt six years earlier, after my unfortunate encounter with those hickory nuts. I knew instantly that the tendon was gone.

I never fully recovered from that first rupture. I had bad feelings about the second one. A surgeon stitched the tendon back together the next day and put me in a soft, removable cast. After a couple of days of inactivity, I was itching to get back to work. I did a few test runs and figured out that even with my left leg immobilized, I could

---

[27]   *After the 2024 election, I emailed our son Jeremy, who had been the only one of our children to foresee the outcome. "I'm bequeathing the title of family seer to you. But beware my son: Uneasy wears the crown. You too will be wrong-footed one day. In fact, many days."*

climb a ladder and resume nailing cedar boards and batons to the exterior of the house. My lifelong friend Lenny, an osteopath, disapproved. I assured him and everyone else that I was a prudent man who put safety first.

I may not have been right about that. One lovely afternoon after I'd gotten myself up onto a flat portion of the roof and was happily hammering away, I ran out of nails. But when I tried to maneuver my way back onto the ladder to get down, I realized I couldn't. The angles didn't work. My body wouldn't let me. Stefanie was off on one of her long daily walks and had warned me not to get up on the roof while she was gone. No one else was around. So there I was, stranded. How stupid can a person get?

Time passed. I stewed. I did my calculations. What would be worse: To be discovered on the roof, helpless and humiliated, in need of a rescue? Or on the ground with more broken body parts, in need of an ambulance? Neither scenario was good. Tentatively, I re-tested various descent strategies. Could I mount the ladder from the left side? From the right side? How much weight could I put on my good leg? My bad leg? Should I remove the cast? Could I trust my balance? After mulling all this for maybe a half hour, I screwed up my courage and somehow hoisted myself onto the top rung of the ladder. And then safely down. To this day I'm not sure how I pulled that off. But I do know this. I'm a jackass. And a lucky one.

My other jackass moment came toward the end of the third summer, when I was midway through building a 53-step stairway that ascends from Stewarts Creek to the new deck James and I had built in the back of the house.

This is my favorite patch of real estate in the world. When I sit on that deck in the morning with a cup of coffee to watch the sun rise over the tops of pine trees, or in the evening with a gin and tonic to dull the day's fresh aches and pains, I look down at the creek and contemplate the magic of nature and march of time. I'm not ordinarily prone to such ruminations. But this little creek captivates me. It's some 40 feet wide and two or three feet deep, a capillary in the vast network of waterways that flow from the Adirondacks Mountains to the Hudson River to the Atlantic Ocean to the far ends of the earth. It moves just fast enough to babble, barely. It's been doing its thing for millions of years. Quietly, relentlessly, unpretentiously, astonishingly, it has carved a valley 50 feet deep into the rolling foothills where our property sits. That little creek!

I spent a lot of time on a lot of ladders! Bad for the knees.

Hammering away with my left leg in a removable cast. Pretty stupid.

Our lot is just four-tenths of an acre. But a world unto itself. Across the creek, which sits to our south, is pristine forest, thick with pine, spruce, maple, birch and hemlock. Every autumn they produce a symphony in greens, golds, reds and yellows. To the east and west are two more tree walls, with the evergreen pines topping out at a majestic 120 feet. When I sit on my deck it's as if I'm suspended in a giant tree house, surrounded by forest on three sides – and, at my back, by the house I helped to build and then to rebuild. I see nothing but nature's handiwork and my own. I hear nothing but the faint ripples of that creek. Every so often, a family of geese floats by or a hawk flies overhead.

I want this spot to be perfect. When we inherited the house, it was a long way from perfect. Decades ago Norm had hired someone to build a stairway down to the creek. Even at its best, it was an ungainly mess – hugging the slope at the top, but, weirdly, suspended on six foot stilts near the bottom. Over the years several of its concrete footers had cracked, so it became a safety hazard. One flight canted left, another right. Stef said it looked like it had been designed and built by Dr. Seuss on acid.

Before we replaced the stairs, James and I built an 8-by-10 foot dock by the side of the creek – big enough for two Adirondack chairs and a small table. As magical as it is to contemplate the creek from above, it's even better down there. You're still in your outdoor room, but the walls are even higher, the ripples louder. And from that vantage point you can watch Stewarts Creek meander all the way to Third Lake, a few hundred feet away.

By the time we finished the dock, summer was over. James, Sarah and their girls headed home for the new school year. I hired a local handyman named Jose to help me with the stairs. The goal was to have them hug the slope all the way up. I did some rough calculations and figured that if we built stairs with 11-inch treads and seven inch risers, we'd get to the top of the slope just where I wanted to – at the base of the steps to the deck that James and I had built two summers before.

Building a 53-step stairway on a steep slope is a hard slog. You have to somehow keep your balance on a 40-degree angle while digging holes, mixing concrete, operating a power saw, and hammering or screwing in the stringers, treads and risers. But Jose and I did good work. (Jose is very sharp). Hundred problems, hundred solutions.

On the afternoon of the second day, we were about halfway up the slope and feeling fine. I decided to double-check my calculations – my thought being that, if necessary, we'd make minor adjustments to the tread/riser scheme the rest of the way up.

It was not merely necessary. It was a fiasco. If we were to stick with that 11/7 tread/riser pattern, we'd burrow into the side of the slope about ten feet below the target. We needed a helluva lot more than a tweak.

This was my worst screw-up of the project. My mistake had been to assume that the slope was on a constant angle. That's how it looked to the naked eye. But in fact, it was steeper in some spots than others, a variation obscured by bushes and underbrush. Aha, that's why Norm's stairs were on stilts at the bottom! His guys must have started at the top and been forced to make their adjustments down below. I'd started from the bottom and now needed to make fixes up top. Apparently this is why people hire engineers.

Jose and I mulled our options. None was good. We could build the remaining stairs in a switch-back pattern, but I didn't want to. I wanted a gently winding stairway that hugged the slope. That's the vision I'd had in my head for three years. That's the way it needed to be.

And that's what I got. I hired Jose's pal Juan to do what he could with a pick and shovel to re-grade the top of the slope. That helped a bit. Then I changed the tread/riser pattern on the remaining steps pretty dramatically – to 9/8 on one of the flights, to 10/8 on the other. This is the last thing you want to do to a staircase. But we had no choice—it was either that or wind up with a set of stairs that tunneled ingloriously into the slope. And all's well that ends well. The following summer James and I built a very sturdy handrail (Two-dimensional miters. Very complicated. All credit to James.) I've since walked up and down those stairs hundreds of times. As long as I clutch that rail,

I'm good. The stairs, deck, dock and creek are exactly where I want them. Best vista in the world. Come see it for yourself! But please, hang on to the banister.

The creek stairs under construction

It all worked out.

Despite these fuck-ups, the biggest challenge we faced on this project wasn't the work. It was the relationship. Never saw that coming. Stef and I are veteran do-it-yourselfers. We have similar tastes. Been married forever. Too smart to fight. Too old to fight.

But we had some nasty ones. Hurtful ones. It turns out our tastes may be in sync, but our work styles are oil and water. She's a planner; I'm an improviser. She tends to go slow; I like to go fast. She's a penny pincher. I say let's get on with it; the pennies will take care of themselves.

This never led to fireworks in the past because Stefanie ran all the projects. This time around, I no longer had a day job, so we ran things together. Big mistake. We fought over how to shop, where to shop, what to buy, how much time to spend cruising the internet looking for better products and lower prices. After two or three websites, I'd hit a wall. Stefanie was just getting started. We also fought over whom to hire and how much to pay them and how to keep track of their time. We fought, too, over the color of the living room wall, the angle of the entryway roof and the size of stones in the retaining wall.

Home remodeling projects are notorious marriage-wreckers. We never got close to becoming the cliché couple that puts the finishing touches on the new kitchen just in time to sign the divorce papers. But our stress levels were right up there. Now that the project is (mostly) done and hostilities have (mostly) receded, it's safe to do an after-action assessment of how things got so out of whack.

We both agree that I won most of the fights simply by bullying ahead. I was in the driver's seat – both literally (Stef doesn't drive) and figuratively (she doesn't use a computer and can't shop online on her own). From Stefanie's perspective, it wasn't just the lopsided won-loss record that was so infuriating. It was her belief that I was railroading her because I thought she couldn't cut it anymore. She was already beating herself up with worry that she was losing agency and control. The last thing she needed was for me to muscle in on her project management turf. This sent her over the top. She accused me of undermining her, sabotaging her, ghosting her. Deliberately. I felt terrible about her situation but was offended by her accusations.

She was telling me I was a really, really bad guy. After all these years! I dug in even deeper.

When we'd get down and dirty, Stef would become super-aggressive. And I'd become super passive-aggressive. She'd reel off a list of my sins, all bunched around a universal theme: "You. Do. Not. Listen." I'd pretend to be too high-minded to rise to my own defense, a pose that the poet Robert Frost once identified as a classic gambit of liberals. "Stef, help me out. I must have done something right in 50 years. One thing!" This would unleash a predictable torrent of fuck-you's from my life partner, occasionally punctuated with a middle finger.

Looking back, Stefanie says her accusations were born of utter exasperation. "I kept trying to get you to listen to me. I kept telling you I didn't like what you were doing. And you kept ignoring me. I needed to get your attention. Nothing else was working."

Our worst fight was about rocks. After we hired an excavator by the name of Rick Carbone to take a big bite out of the slope in front of the house to make room for the new portico I was about to build, we needed to keep the gouged-out section from eroding. Rick said he could build a retaining wall with boulders from a nearby quarry. He drove us to a home a few towns away so we could take a look at a similar wall he'd built.

The two of us talked it over that night.

I said: "This'll be great. The rocks will complement the cedar siding. Rustic against rustic. Perfect!"

Stef said: "It'll look like a fucking road construction project. Next to a ski chalet."

I said: "We gotta keep the slope back somehow. You got a better idea?"

Stef said: "We're in New York, not Colorado."

I said: "But we gotta keep the slope back somehow."

And so on. We never settled the issue.

The War of the Rocks started here.

The next day I went ahead and hired him. His boulders were bigger than I'd expected – four to five thousand pounds apiece. But sitting in the cab of his excavator, working his levers like a kid at the arcade, he was a maestro.[28] His first order of business was to line up two walls of boulders like strings of pearls to enclose a new curved stairway to the new portico. One of his crew members would wrap a chain around each boulder, which Rick would then lift with the bucket of his excavator, dangle over the drop zone, then slowly lower to the designated spot, at just the right pitch and angle, miraculously without crushing the hands of the two sidekicks who guided the descent and tweaked the final placement. I was mesmerized by the choreography and astonished that no one lost a finger. Once those two walls were in place, they deposited dozens more smaller boulders to hold back the rest of the slope they'd created. The following summer I purchased a load of smaller rocks and built a waterfall [29] alongside our new curved stairway. And still more rocks to define the edges of our semi-circular driveway. I hauled, laid and placed something like 25,000 pounds of rocks that summer. To passers-by who observed me at my labors, I would raise my arms triumphantly and proclaim: I am a rock star!

The Adirondacks are a relatively young mountain range – mere tens of millions of years old – but they're made of rocks that have been around for more than a billion years. I have a soft spot for rocks. "The voice of stone is an echo from the depths of time," dry

---

[28] *Rick Carbone is a charming and dapper 76-year-old who tools around on his Harley or in his red Corvette when he's not in the cab of his excavator or one of his other trucks. He's made a great living in road construction and gets too big a kick from work to retire. Half a century ago, Norm and Bea hired him to dig the holes and set in the cinder block piers for the home they were about to build. Rick also built them their glorious stone fireplace, using skills he'd inherited from his stone mason dad. Everyone loves a stone fireplace. Rick built the best one in the world. And the best retaining wall. Same guy did 'em both, 50 years apart, for the same house. How cool is that?*

[29] *I have a thing for waterfalls —the look, the sound. One of them — Rockwell Falls in Lake Luzerne, the narrowest stretch of the Hudson River — is where Stef and I first held hands. And at our house in Bethesda, I've built a small waterfall in the front yard, a big one in the back yard and a medium-sized one in the family room. People think I'm a little nuts. They may have a point.*

waller Dan Snow wrote in his enchanting book, *Listening to Stone.* He doesn't go as far as novelist Thomas Pynchon, who suspects that rocks have thoughts and feelings. But he does believe "they hold a muscle memory of all their earthly experience." Snow also sees a connection between writing and walling. He quotes a letter from author and essayist E.B White: "We are having splendid weather and I am building a stone wall. I understand that all literary people, at one time or another, build a stone wall. It's because it's easier than writing."[30] My literary efforts don't inhabit the same universe as those of White, Pynchon or Snow, but I second their sentiments. And I love listening to my rocks.

Stefanie hates them. No, let me amend that. She hated them at first. She merely dislikes them now. She still thinks they make the place look like a fucking ski chalet. Or a highway embankment. Or both. But we've done a few things to take some pus out of the boil. We hired a metal fabricator to create a curved banister that he drilled into the stairway boulders. We painted it a deep Adirondack green. We painted the cement stairs a rich rust color. We painted the front door our trademark turquoise. The overall effect is cool/funky/rustic/whimsical, which delights us both. No, not a classic Adirondack cabin. But not a fucking Colorado ski chalet either! Nothing like it anywhere.

Stef has made an uneasy peace with it. What she can't abide – what she'll never get over – is the way I blew past her and did it all my way. In retrospect, I have no defense. I was sure I was right. We had a project to finish. I was frustrated with Stef. I got on with it.

I knew at the time I was out of line, but I didn't realize how much. One of the unspoken rules of our marriage is that we never do anything important unless both of us are on board. I broke that compact.

---

[30] *So true! There are a thousand ways to build a paragraph. And a thousand ways to build a wall. But once you've built your wall, you're heavily disincentivized to change it, whereas you can spend the rest of your life fixing that goddamn paragraph.*

I didn't see it that way at the time because I'd managed to convince myself that what we were arguing about wasn't all that important. I didn't realize how hurtful this was for Stefanie because I wasn't accounting for the weight of her anxieties or the anger that wells up when you've been ignored. This was me being obtuse. And in denial. I don't want her to be someone with anxieties. I want her to be the same kick ass free spirit I fell in love with half a century ago. She's astonishingly good at compensating for her vision and movement disabilities. So good that nobody realizes how exhausting it is. I'm good about driving her to places and helping her now and then with some of the adjustments she needs to make to get through the day. But I'm no good at helping her cope with her anxieties. I'm not wired that way. It wasn't part of the deal when we were young. I think she spends too much time worrying about things that will take care of themselves. I think she'd be happier if she worried less; so would I. But try telling a worrier not to worry. Take it from me, it doesn't go well. So I gotta work on that. As for her, she ought to be able to see my blind spot for what it is – insensitive, not malicious. Gotta work on that.

In his book *Supercommunicators,* Charles Duhigg writes that a common source of trouble in a marriage comes when you and your spouse aren't on the same page about the nature of the fight you're having. One partner wants a venting session. The other partner wants a problem-solving session. One is battle ready; the other conflict averse. So you talk past each other. Many couples have these sorts of fights, even happily married ones. And all couples have scar tissue, even happily married ones. A good survival technique, Duhigg writes, is for both partners to try to make each fight as small as possible. Don't let it reopen old wounds. Stay in the moment. And if possible, don't make the fight about what's wrong with your partner. Make it about what you can do to make things better.

Wise words. Stef and I are working on it. Happily, we're back to being best buds. But the tension that had cast a pall over the whole adventure still crops up whenever we revisit some of the dust-ups.

That's too bad, because when you finish a huge project like this, it's fun to celebrate all the war stories – triumphs, fuck-ups, near misses, great saves. James and I do this all the time, to much mutual merriment: the impossible-to-assemble sliding glass door; the 140 square foot shim we improvised under the new dining room floor; the leaning-tower- of- Pisa column we had to fix under the deck; the lost specialty washer that nearly derailed a whole afternoon's work – until we miraculously found it under a bush when it was illuminated by the reflection of the setting sun. We love yanking each other's chains about our different relationships with tools. James has a zillion of them. I'm old school. Gimme a hammer, a saw and a screwdriver – I'm good to go. At least that's how I was at the outset. In our first summer working together, I'd roll my eyes each time James dug into his tool box for another exotic power saw or more of those funny-shaped screw-head bits to attach to his endless supply of power screwdrivers. But I also noticed that he was better and faster than me at everything. By year two I started playing around with some of his big-boy toys. By year three I had no idea how I'd ever survived without them. James enjoys reminding me of my journey.

With Stefanie and me, it's all still too fraught for this sort of amusement. We'll take some of our arguments to the grave. But just as surely, we'll take with us a sense of awe at what we managed to pull off at this stage of life, despite being pissed off at each other much of the time.

By the way, I didn't win all the fights. The dining room is a rectangle, not a triangle. Stefanie was bang on right about that one. Had we gone with my plan, we would have needed a triangular table too.

CHAPTER NINE

SCENES FROM A MARRIAGE

Have I left the impression that these were the only fights we had in 50-plus years of marriage? Well let's clear that up. In fact, we got off to a shaky start. How shaky? How's this: For the first few months, Stef had a packed suitcase parked next to the front door of our apartment. Subtle, right?

At the time we were living in Winston-Salem, N.C., where I was starting my journalism career at The Twin City Sentinel. Stefanie had taken enough courses at the New School in New York City to earn her BA from SUNY-Albany.[31] Right after that we got married in her parents' Brooklyn living room in front of a small gathering of family and friends. I had promised to compose our wedding vows but came down with a bad case of writer's block. Mercifully, our officiant – an Ethical Culture Society minister we'd met the week before – bailed

---

[31]   *I helped write some of her papers. Talk about love!*

me out.[32] The ceremony came off just fine. All the wedding guests said the minister was eloquent. I told them I'd helped him compose the vows (not strictly a lie; I did suggest a few phrases that made the cut), but sorry, no, we didn't have a written version. Stef and I agree that the person who enjoyed the day the most was her elderly immigrant grandmother, who was no longer in possession of all her marbles. She slept through most of it. Periodically she would wake up and ask Stef. "Where am I? What's all the commotion?" "I'm getting married Grandma." "Wonderful! Is he Jewish?" "Yes." Wonderful!!!" Then she'd fall back to sleep. A half dozen more times that afternoon, she'd wake up, have the identical conversation with Stef, then doze off again. I don't remember much about our wedding other than how happy we'd made Stef's grandmother. And that never in my life – before or since – have I gotten so much credit for being Jewish.

We spent our wedding night at the Waldorf Astoria, then headed up to Fourth Lake for a short honeymoon. After that, we drove south to start our married life. We were 21 years old and madly in love. But there were issues.

At least initially, Stef was a fish out of water – a big city Northern girl in a sleepy Southern town. I had preceded her by six months in Winston-Salem and was having a ball as a general assignment reporter, covering cops and courts and zoning boards and sewer commissions, an ideal apprenticeship for my craft. Eventually Stef would get a job in the child protection division of the Forsyth County Social Services Department, and the two of us would become live-in "parents" at a temporary receiving home for children who were emergency wards of the county. But it took her a while to land that job. For her first

---

[32]   *I phoned him the Saturday morning of the wedding to warn him that I hadn't written the vows. This was a humiliating phone call to make. But, as it turned out, it saved my ass. He assured me this wouldn't be a problem. "Okay great, thanks, I'll see you this afternoon." "What do you mean this afternoon? I thought the wedding was tomorrow! I was about to play golf." Life is funny, no? Best writer's block I ever had.*

few months in this alien habitat, she was a waitress. She didn't mind the work (I used to leave her great tips!) but was antsy to get on with a career in social work.

It didn't help that we had different ideas about how to amuse ourselves. If memory serves, that packed suitcase first materialized near the front door on a balmy Sunday afternoon that Stef wanted to spend with me outdoors while I pointed out that there was a football game on TV that needed watching.

Things eventually got better. We fell in with a great group of friends – reporters, artists, writers, professors.[33] And they, along with what turned out to be fascinating jobs for both of us, made those two and a half years in Winston-Salem quite wonderful.

You don't get into journalism to get rich. My starting salary was $126 a week. We paid $70-a-month to live in a sketchy part of town. It was in an old house that had been converted into four small apartments, two up and two down. Our downstairs neighbors were Boots[34] and Gladys. He was a house painter, she a waitress. They were in their 40s, but both could have easily passed for 60. Nice folks when sober, which wasn't often. When drunk, they'd get rough with each other. At night, I'd periodically hear shouting, thumping, crashing. Sometimes Gladys would start wailing: "Taylor! Taylor! Help me Taylor. He's beating me, Taylor!" I'd go downstairs. They'd let me in, chastened, sheepish and seemingly no worse for wear. The only time anyone got seriously hurt, it turned out to be Boots. "Taylor, this time we really need you!! Come quick!" I went downstairs to find Boots'

---

[33] *Rick Edmonds started his career as a reporter in Winston-Salem the same summer I did. We both got married soon after. He and his wife Marianne have been dear friends ever since. Rick was a superb reporter who battled diabetes, heart problems, mobility issues and assorted other ailments. He died at age 78 when a mattress blew off the top of the car traveling in front of his on a busy highway near his home in Florida. He was being driven by an aide to an exercise class. Life can be so random. Death too.*

[34] *Boots had a twin brother whose name, of course, was Toots.*

right thumb barely attached to his hand. They said he'd had an accident. It was pretty obvious that Gladys must have lunged at him with a kitchen knife, which he'd grabbed before she could shove it into his stomach. I drove them to the ER, where he had the thumb stitched back on. In a matter of weeks, they were back to their nightly fights. The odd thing is that, through it all, they seemed to genuinely care for each other. Often at night, after the roughhousing was over, I'd hear Boots strumming on his guitar and belting out his favorite country tune in a sweet and mournful voice: "Please release me, let me go. I don't love you anymore. To live together is a sin. Release me and let me love again." Sometimes Gladys would sing along.

For much of our stay in Winston-Salem, we only lived in that apartment every other weekend. The rest of the time we lived on the grounds of the Memorial Industrial School, an orphanage in nearby Rural Hall, N.C. It was there that Stefanie ran a temporary receiving home for children who had come into the custody of the county's child protective service division, sometimes under horrific circumstances. Stef had a sixth sense about how best to comfort them – who needed hugs, who needed space. In a couple of instances, we took in kids whose father had just killed their mother. Once it was a family of six siblings, dropped off late at night by a social worker and the police. We soothed them as best we could and put them to sleep in six beds. In the morning, we found all six huddled together in one bed. Good God, I remember thinking, I hope they give each other that kind of support for the rest of their lives.

Our home had a rapid turnover by design; our kids stayed only for a matter of days, sometimes weeks, while Stefanie worked with their social workers to organize a long-term placement. The orphanage, by contrast, was full of kids who had been there for most of their young lives. This was a segregated facility; everyone else – kids and staff – was black. We were quite the curiosity. I remember how fascinated the kids were by our hair – straight and blonde for Stefanie; curly but not kinky for me. Every now and then, one would screw up his or her courage and ask to touch our hair. We'd say sure, but could we also touch yours? On some days I'd shoot baskets or play ball with the orphanage kids. One of my fondest memories is the afternoon I got home from work to find that Stef had already organized a baseball game. The grounds of the orphanage covered 500 acres. It had just one paved road. That's where Stef had set up first base, second base, third base and home plate. You can take the girl out of Brooklyn; you can't take Brooklyn out of the girl.

Our time at that home gave us something of a coming-attractions reel about parenthood. We both knew right away we'd be good at it. I knew Stef would be great at it. There's a gaping hole in this memoir, because we agreed from the get-go that I wouldn't write about our kids. They are by far the best part of our lives. Each of them has a wonderful family. But their stories are theirs to tell, not ours. I will, however, say this: My children and I all share one extraordinary stroke of luck. We all grew up with the best mommy in the world.

Stefanie nursing Jeremy, our first-born.

Our young family on the beach at Fourth Lake.

When Stefanie and I started having kids, our marriage got both easier and harder. Easier because when it comes to child-rearing, we've always been on the same page – our values, instincts, norms and styles are in sync. And because our kids provided us with something our marriage hadn't had until then – a magnificent shared project. Harder because raising children is really hard! And because we weren't wired to share the burden equally. I was the breadwinner; Stefanie was the homemaker. We both understood she had the more difficult job.

That marital arrangement sounds old-fashioned now. Even back then, it was falling out of favor. Among our married friends throughout our child-rearing years, Stef was an outlier. Most of the other young mothers we knew had careers. This was an era when the "mommy wars" (working moms versus stay-at-home moms) made for vivid copy and occasionally angry diatribes in general circulation magazines and feminist tracts. Stef was a non-combatant. She was happy with her choice; she was cool with everyone else's choices. "I always knew it would be hard for me to quote/unquote 'have it all,' and I had no interest in trying."

Some clever person once said that marriages start in rhapsodies and end in carpools. Stef and I survived those carpool years, but we had our moments. Whenever I was on the road for one of my long trips covering presidential candidates, I'd try to phone home every night around 7 p.m. so I could talk to the kids before they went to sleep. None of us ever felt very good about those conversations. They were flat and formulaic. "How was school? What did you have for supper?" The longer I was away the flatter they got. Stef remembers one of our young sons asking her if daddy was really alive. "Of course," she said. "You talk to him every night on the phone." "Mommy," he replied, "they have machines that can do that." (This was four decades before ChatGPT. Smart kid!)

All three of our kids were born in Philadelphia, where I worked for the Inquirer during its golden age under its charismatic editor, Gene Roberts. Stefanie and I became close friends with a bunch of other young reporters and spouses who, like us, were just starting families. For the past half century, our Philly gang has reconvened in one of our homes every New Years Eve, where we feast on an elaborate home-cooked meal that's always brought to a closing crescendo by Stef's to-die-for Chocolate Three Bomb Cake. We missed a few of these galas during Covid. When we reconnected in 2024, it was like slipping into an old shoe that still fits perfectly. Some things do change, of course. We used to talk about our kids. Now we talk about our grandkids.

When I left the Inquirer to join the Washington Post in 1981, our oldest was six and our youngest was a newborn. Raising a young family as the stay-at-home-wife of a Washington Post political reporter brought no end of adventures for Stef. I used to get invited to parties where politicians, lobbyists, PR people, diplomats and reporters pretended to be chums while each of us worked whatever angles we were working. Sometimes spouses were invited. I recall one invitation to an intimate dinner for a dozen. "There is no agenda," I was assured in an elegant font on embossed stationery, "other than to have a good time." The host helpfully enclosed an addendum with the names and CVs of all the guests. I had little appetite for these evenings; Stefanie even less. But as a good sport, and always with an anthropologist's eye, she would occasionally tag along. Some people were charmed by her; others were confused. Or worse. She remembers going to one party after she'd been tiling our kitchen all day and hadn't had any luck washing the dark grout out from her fingernails. "People didn't know what to make of me." But even without the visual tells, she was a rare and disorienting creature. "The first thing people would ask me is what I did for a living. When I'd tell them I was raising our children, they were baffled. When I'd say I'd been spending a lot of time with plumbers because I was renovating a bathroom, I'd count the seconds until they excused themselves and looked for someone else to chat up."

Over the course of our marriage, we've lived in a bunch of different places: Winston-Salem, Philadelphia, Bethesda, Austin, Johannesburg and of course Fourth Lake. We loved 'em all; made lifelong friends at every stop. We're both good at adapting to new environments, but it's Stef who brings the special sauce. She's a social magnet; a superb hostess; the best of friends to make and easiest to keep.

We entertain a lot. Some couples remember the great restaurants where they've dined. We remember the great dinners we've hosted. The first of them was in Winston Salem, a culinary backwater at the time. It took Stef and several co-conspirators several days and many miles to round up the ingredients for an elaborate beef bourguignon meal they were determined to prepare. They were all new to this. Their attempt to bake French bread produced a variation on the bagel. And they badly miscalculated how long it would take to put all the courses together. There were eight of us in our tiny apartment. We started eating at around 7 p.m. I think we served the main course at around 12:30 a.m. Very cool.

Then there was the first dinner party we threw in Johannesburg, not long after I got shot. We invited lots of people. Lots of people came (Hey, briefly, I was famous!). In short order we were schooled on several local customs. 1. The Afrikaners showed up at the stroke of 6 p.m. The Africans started filtering in at around 9 p.m. The hacks and expats arrived in between. 2. Many guests brought their kids. 3. We had way too much food and way too little booze. This was on a Sunday; the liquor stores were closed. Early in the proceedings, when we saw where things were headed, we put out an emergency call to a few friends. They rescued us by bringing many extra bottles of wine. We did better the next time.

The most elaborate meal Stef ever cooked was for our daughter's wedding. Stefanie prepared an exquisite five-course dinner that would be the envy of any Michelin-rated restaurant. I can produce the menu here because we printed it, along with all the recipes, in a booklet we handed out as a party favor. **Starters:** Chevre & Phyllo Kisses; Pate Mousse with Bacon & Walnuts; Chicken Satay with Peanut Sauce; Hummus; Pigs in a Blanket; Herbed Shrimp with Snow Peas. **Soup:** Thai Cucumber Soup. **Main Courses:** Ginger Honey Salmon; Beef Tenderloin with Horse Radish Sauce. **Sides:** Lemony Couscous;

Waldorf Salad. **Desserts:** Chocolate Cheesecake; Lemon Ginger Cheesecake: Chocolate Fondue. Stef prepared this feast with the help of a handful of girlfriends. We hired a small waitstaff to serve it as sit-down dinner. For 125! I was in charge of logistics. I rented a bunch of tables and chairs; moved a lot of our furniture into the garage; and converted every downstairs room and three upstairs bedrooms into makeshift dining rooms. I set up a few more tables outside. Viola! Sit-down dinner for 125, Chez Stefanie.[35]

Over the years in Bethesda, we've hosted hundreds of dinner parties, though only twice for so many guests. The vibes at our soirees could not be more different from what goes down at those Inside-the-Beltway preening festivals. Because the vibes are all Stef. Dress casually. Clear your own plates. Schmooze about politics, sure, but let's also talk about kids, books, movies, TV shows, recipes, restaurants, vacations, and – everyone's guilty pleasure – house prices. If you've got an angle you're looking to play, you've come to the wrong party.

Our most memorable dinner guest was Teddy Kennedy. He was invited by a mutual friend who knew him from Martha's Vinyard. Stef and I aren't shrinking violets, but this was intimidating. We'd grown up at a time when the popular culture was steeped in all things Kennedy and Camelot – the glamour, mystique, wealth, tragedy. Hosting the lone surviving brother for dinner felt out of our league. In the days leading up to the party, I kept reassuring Stef: "Don't worry, he's probably not coming. The Senate has a busy agenda; it's been staying in session late into the night for votes. Plus, he's not going to want to haul out to Bethesda on a weeknight for a dinner that isn't a fundraiser, hosted by a couple he doesn't know." On the morning of the dinner, Stef called me at work. "We're fucked. I just got a call

---

[35] *When one of our sons got married a few years later, we mounted a similar feast. Our other son took his vows in Manhattan City Hall.*

from a guy on Kennedy's staff. He wants directions to the house and the names of the other guests so they could do a security check."

The dinner was a rollicking success. This was a few years before Kennedy got sick with brain cancer. He was in full-throated, tub-thumping Lion-of-the-Senate mode, mesmerizing all of us around the table with one funny story after another about the inanities of politics. At one point, as he swung out his arms for emphasis, he toppled the wine glass of the dinner guest to his left, a federal appeals court judge who happens to be blind. Everyone froze. We took a moment to clean up the table. Someone made a crack about the sighted guy knocking over the blind guy's glass. Then Teddy roared ahead with more stories.

The next morning Stefanie answered the phone. It was Ted's wife Reggie, calling to say what a wonderful time they'd had. Stef said it was an honor to have hosted them and agreed it was great fun. She added, "A lot of alpha males around the table. None of the women could get in a word edgewise." At which point Ted erupted in laughter. Stef hadn't realized he was also on the call. "Yeah," the Lion of the Senate agreed, "Reggie tells me I need to work on that."

I've got one more name to drop: Jose Andres, the chef, restaurateur and humanitarian. He too was invited to our house by a mutual friend; this time the meal was brunch. The only thing we'd been told in advance was that his name was Jose. He brought along his three-year old daughter. She spent much of the meal bouncing on his lap. At one point Jose produced his own small knife, sliced an apple into segments and fed them to his daughter from the tip of that knife. This unnerving but deft little move set off a light switch for Stefanie and me. We repaired to the kitchen. "Holy shit," Stefanie whispered. "That's Jose Andres!" He was already celebrity chef back then; but not yet the global champion of humanitarian food aid he has since become. Every year when we write a check to his World Central Kitchen, we think of him joyfully feeding his daughter with the tip of his knife.

If anybody ever brings up his name, we're happy to tell them: "Great guy. Had him over for brunch back when he was starting out."

For a brief spell, food became something more to Stefanie than just the anchor of our social life. "I'll Bring Dessert" was the name of her one-woman catering service. It didn't last long. Baking cakes and pies for strangers turned out not to be her thing. In time she moved on to a more successful one-woman enterprise: jewelry making. She has a flair for the craft, with a style influenced by two of the places we've lived, Africa and the American Southwest. She uses mixed metals (mostly silver and gold) and colorful stones (mostly turquoise and amethyst). She's partial to big pieces, be they earrings or necklaces or bracelets. When she first studied jewelry-making in Africa, she had no ambition other than to wear what she'd made. But people kept admiring her pieces and asking where she'd bought them. When she'd tell them, they'd ask if she'd make something for them. So Stef started selling jewelry to friends, then friends of friends, and so on. But she never developed a sales strategy beyond word-of-mouth. She had no website, no social media presence, no patience for booths at craft fairs, not even so much as a business card. Frankly, it's never been clear she's ever really wanted to sell anything to anybody. There's not a molecule of entrepreneurial DNA in her family tree. I used to kid her that if she ever decided to print a business card, it should read: "I Make Jewelry. You Can't Have It." Eventually she came around to displaying her work at a co-op gallery in Bethesda for local artists and craftspeople. She had to leave the gallery a few years ago when her vision deteriorated to the point that she could no longer make any new work. In her prime, year in and year out, her business was never brisk. Just how she liked it.

As you've no doubt already gleaned, Stefanie and I have different tolerances for risk. Imagine the following familiar scenario: You're driving your car and the traffic light at the intersection just ahead turns yellow. There are two ways you can interpret this information. As a warning to slow down. Or as an encouragement to speed up. Suffice it to say: Stef and I do not process yellow lights the same way. And yes, this is a metaphor.

But it's also a literal trouble spot. Everyone knows that the automobile can be the angriest of marital battlegrounds. Stef and I have had more than our share of back-seat-driver fights. I won't bore you with them, because we also have a more exotic car problem. We have wholly different belief systems about when you need to refill the gas tank.

As the loving daughter of risk-averse parents, Stefanie was raised to believe that when the gas gauge falls all the way down to half, you damn well better refill it. I grew up with a different coda. Our family had two cars; the second was an inexpensive clunker that was good only for short trips around town. By the time I got my driver's license, my brother was away at college. That second car was shared by my mom and me. And we reveled in playing an undeclared game of chicken. The goal was to make sure you didn't get stuck having to refill the tank. And if you did get stuck, you wanted to keep the hit to your wallet as light as possible. Every time I had to fill up, I'd put in one dollar's worth. Back then that got you three gallons. Mom would do the same thing. As a result, we'd each run out of gas with some regularity. But since neither of us ever drove that car outside the neighborhood, this was a minor inconvenience. A cost of doing business. In fact, kind of fun.

I brought this strange attitude about empty gas tanks with me to college. In my senior year I moved off campus and bought an old jalopy so I could make the commute from East Haven to New Haven. Stefanie would visit me every weekend. One night when we were on a road trip to I can't remember where, we ran out of gas. "Fuck," Stef said, "the goddamn gas gauge must be broken." I considered other explanations but realized I had no good play but to confess. It did not go well. Stefanie looked at me as if I were nuts. Happily, we weren't far from a gas station. Even better, I've reformed. There have been a few lapses over the years. But I'm old and conservative now. I can barely remember the last time I ran out of gas.

My most daring game of risk – and in retrospect, my dumbest – came the day before that glorious home wedding we threw for our daughter. Our plan was for the afternoon ceremony to take place on our lawn, followed by an outdoor cocktail hour. For dinner, some of our guests would be seated inside, some outside. After dinner, everyone would head outside and dance under the stars. I had gotten it in my head that the look and feel of this auspicious production would be much better if we didn't use a tent, which I've always found a bit claustrophobic at such events. Stef agreed but insisted we have one available in case there was rain in the forecast. I said: Of course. So we rented a big party tent with a proviso that we could cancel without penalty up to 48 hours in advance. Two days out, the forecast looked dicey, so we told the tent people we needed it. The next day, the forecast improved. The chance of rain fell to 30 percent. To me, 30% means it's probably not going to rain. To Stef, it means something different. Toward the end of that day, the rain chance was down to 20%. At which point I called the tent people and told them I didn't want them to set it up. They said I'd still have to pay for it because we were beyond the cancellation deadline. I told them yup, no worries, I understood. Stefanie was furious. But she was so preoccupied preparing that meal for 125 people, she barely had time to vent.

The morning of the wedding broke under a bright June sun. Then around 10 a.m. some clouds rolled in. It started raining at around 11 a.m. The wedding was scheduled for 4 p.m. We had about a dozen friends and relatives with us during the morning, helping put the finishing touches on the meal and the lawn. Everyone went into a mild panic. Except for me. Mine was not mild.

I consulted the Weather Channel. "It looks like this will stop at around noon," I announced, shakily. Stef had just returned from her morning run. She was soaked from the rain and unimpressed with my forecast. "If it doesn't, we're going to have a wedding and a divorce on the same day."

It stopped raining just after noon. The wedding was a smashing success. Lovely outdoor ceremony, unforgettable five-course dinner, dancing till midnight under the stars. Everyone had a blast.

And that, ladies and gents, is one of our secrets to a long and happy marriage. You do your thing. Your spouse does her thing. And you catch some breaks with the weather.

We sometimes ask ourselves now: How did we know as 21-year-olds that we'd find this equipoise? That we'd chosen the right partners? That we'd make it for the long haul? We didn't. We were in love. We took a leap.

A character in Anne Tyler's novel *A Patchwork Planet* describes the secret to long marriages this way: "I knew couples who'd been married almost forever – forty, fifty, sixty years. Seventy-two in one case. They'd be tending each other's illnesses, filling in each other's faulty memories, dealing with the money troubles or the daughter's suicide or the grandson's drug addiction. And I was beginning to suspect that it made no difference whether they'd married the right person. Finally, you're just with who you're with. You signed on with her, put in half a century with her, grown to know her as well as you know yourself or even better, and she's *become* the right person. Or the only person, might be more to the point."

To my ears, those words get the carpools but miss the rhapsodies. Better, I think, is the way psychologist Erich Fromm described enduring love. He said it is a mixture of feelings and behaviors, constantly tended. "It is the active concern for the life and growth of that which we love."

Had I read Fromm back in 1970, would I have borrowed his words for the wedding vows I never managed to write? I doubt it. That young man knew everything about falling in love. He knew nothing about staying in love.

This old man knows both. Lucky me.

CHAPTER TEN

THE FIELD NARROWS

January, 2024

About four years ago Stefanie was reading childrens' books to Sabine, who was 7 at the time, and Clementine, then 5. After Stef finished one, they handed her another. This one had a smaller type size.

"Sorry girls. Grandma can't read this one," she told them. "The words are too small."

"Don't worry Grandma," Sabine comforted. "Relax. Take a breath. You got this!"

Of all the reactions Stef has had to her vision problems, that's her favorite. In Sabine's defense, she's not the only person confused about what her grandmother can and cannot see. Just about everyone is, including me.

Glaucoma is a progressive disease that occurs when elevated levels of pressure from fluids in the back of the eye damage the optic nerve. It is the leading cause of low vision and blindness in adults. There is no cure. The only goal of treatment – which can take the form of medication or surgery or both – is to slow or stop the progression. Stefanie's glaucoma doesn't respond well to medication. So she's had two dozen surgeries, some by laser, most by knife.

In the dozen years since her diagnosis, she's been in a hazy limbo between sighted and blind. She compensates so well that her problems are easy to miss, which is how she's always wanted it. But her symptoms have steadily worsened, slowly at first, more rapidly in recent years. In the past several months they've taken an especially ominous turn.

For the first time, she's thinking about learning to tap with a cane. She's not sure how much it will help her get around. Nor is she sure if she wants to publicly advertise her low vision. But she began pondering both questions last September, after her visit with an optometrist named Suleiman Alibhai, who specializes in helping patients cope with low vision. Alibhai is highly regarded; it had taken nearly a year to get the appointment.

Which turned out to be a revelation. Once he completed the familiar battery of eye tests, Alibhai asked her: "How did you get here?"

"I walked," Stefanie said. She explained that we live less than a mile from his office.

"That's astonishing. You must be exhausted. I am in awe of what you're able to do."

"I knew right away this guy got me," Stef told me later.

What Alibhai knew immediately is something I've been slow to understand: Low vision is exhausting! You spend every waking minute on workarounds. Sometimes they can be pretty straightforward, especially when you're in a familiar space. But even then, you're "on" all the time. You never know when the next open cabinet door will attack. Or when someone puts the yogurt back on the wrong refrigerator shelf, where you can't find it. It's worse when you're on unfamiliar terrain – a restaurant, a supermarket, a dimly-lit sidewalk, a crowded intersection, a house or office you've never visited before. You can get discombobulated in the blink of an eye.

Stefanie is fearless, relentless, anxious, resourceful. She does her coping beneath everyone's radar. Last summer I finally got a small sense of what low vision is like when I had eye surgery to correct a tear in my retina. The operation went fine but five months later, my depth perception is still slightly off. I'm tentative behind the steering wheel. I'm a disaster on a tennis court. It takes my brain a split second too long to figure out how fast a ball is coming at me, so I'll occasionally whiff. Weird! The silver lining is that at least I have a better feel for what Stef lives with every day, though her symptoms are way worse.

During Stefanie's visit with Alibhai, he recommended she learn to tap with a cane. "It'll be like an extension of your hand. You don't have to use it all the time. Just when you feel you need it. If you find yourself in a crowded place and you're uncomfortable, unfold it. The seas will part."

The two of them traded stories about dealing with people who don't know how to deal with people with low vision. "Someone will show me a picture on their cell phone and I'll say, 'Sorry I can't see that.' So they'll lean in and put the phone a little closer to my face. I used to say, 'Oh, yes, how lovely.' Lately I've begun to say, 'No, I still can't see that.'"

"Put me in the camp of people who can't believe you have as little vision as you do," Alibhai told her.

But to complicate the psychological landscape, Stef said she sometimes feels like a fraud talking about her vision problems. "It's not that I can't see. It's that I can't see very well."

For the past few years, whenever Stef has used walking sticks to help her with her movement and vision issues, she's attracted attention, some of it creepy. "When I'm out on the walking trail, I'll get these older guys hitting on me. 'Hard core!' 'Go for it!' 'Cool sticks!' 'Do they really work?'" For a while she was also wearing an eye patch, adding to her allure. She finds the encounters annoying and amusing. "I'm thinking, 'Really?' And I'm thinking, 'Fuuuuck.'!"

As her symptoms have gotten worse, Stefanie has accumulated lots of gizmos. In the kitchen – her lair – she relies on several different magnifying devices, a high intensity task light, and cutting boards of different colors. She's put brightly colored duct tape at strategic spots on various kitchen appliances to signal the settings she uses. We now have big screen TVs in both of our houses; most of the time, she can make out what's going on. She's a voracious reader who had to give up books a few years ago. She now reads exclusively on a tablet, where she can amp up the type to whatever size she needs. She doesn't have the patience for audio books.

There are lots of software programs for folks with low vision, but Stefanie doesn't use them. Astonishingly, she has never used a computer. Or email. Or social media. Or a smart phone. Yup, my wife is a digital luddite. Proud of it.

A few weeks after the visit with Alibhai, her eyesight took a sharp turn for the worse. In early October, she had to have emergency surgery because the pressure in her right eye had risen to a level that was doing further damage to the optic nerve. Following the surgery, there were all sorts of complications. A pool of blood got trapped behind the retina of her surgery eye, rendering it useless. A plastic drain that had been implanted in the eye didn't function properly, leading to pressure readings that alternated between dangerously low and dangerously high.

Stef had to have follow-up surgery a week later. Two weeks after that, she had *another* follow-up surgery. Throughout that whole awful month, she was in constant pain: "It felt like I had a piece of glass in my eye." Most likely, it was a stitch on her eyeball that took a long time to dissolve. As the blood clot finally started to dissipate, her vision played the strangest tricks. Some days she would see spiders out of her surgery eye. Some days diagonal lines. Some days wavy lines. Some days fireworks. When she started to see actual images, they were half the size of the images she saw out of her other eye. One day when we were in the car, stopped at an intersection, she announced:

"I can see the stop sign! But inside the stop sign, I see another stop sign!" That's when she started wearing an eye patch.

For most of that month, she was grounded by her doctors. They told her it wasn't yet safe to take her daily walks. This drove her a wee bit crazy: "My body is turning into a marshmallow!" When she was finally set free, she at first took the precaution of walking around the block rather than taking her usual outing on the nearby Bethesda Crescent Trail. This too drove her slightly nuts. "Twenty loops around the same block! That'll drive anyone crazy. And I keep losing count."

For a brief spell I joined her for those walks – something that, in fifty years, I've rarely done. One thing Stef prizes most about her walks is the solitude. She spends the time working out the day's problems. She doesn't want company.

Under the circumstances, though, I figured she could use some moral support. And a bit of physical help. Stef agreed to leave her sticks behind and latch onto my arm for guidance. A new arrangement for both of us. She proceeded to amuse and alarm me with a stream of mordant banter.

"You're fucked. You're glued to a catastrophe. Get out now!"

"Not gonna happen. I signed up for the whole trip."

"I don't want you to have to take care of me. I don't want that to be how you remember me. And you won't be very good at it."

"I probably won't be any good. But who knows, maybe I'll surprise you."

"I've become my parents."

"It's not that bad."

"Did you ever think you'd grow up to be my chauffer and designated walker?"

"Didn't see that coming."

"Look at the bright side: You don't need to bring a poop bag. At least not yet."

"Definitely a plus."

"If I'm going blind how come I can still see all my wrinkles?"

"X-ray vision."

Stef's right eye has finally healed from the complications of that latest round of surgeries, so she's no longer in pain. But her vision has never been worse. In one eye she has limited field – "like looking through a periscope." In the other, poor acuity – "like looking at someone in the witness protection program." Neither eye works well on its own. The two of them don't play nicely with each other.

Yesterday we saw the retina specialist who now treats us both. His-and-her-back-to-back appointments. Lovely! He had mildly encouraging news for me. Within three to six months I should fully recover from my eye surgery, at which point I'll be a candidate for cataract surgery. Assuming that goes well, I ought to be smacking the tennis ball like a pro. Alrighty!

Stef's prognosis was not good. He said the glaucoma is relentless and it's winning. And it's probably going to keep on winning. He and all of Stef's eye docs will keep doing everything they can. But we should plan accordingly.

When you get that kind of news, especially after you've had a round of surgeries that obviously didn't go as planned, there's a temptation to question the quality of your medical care. Stef and I have sometimes gone down that rabbit hole. But only briefly. The Wilmer Eye Institute is regarded as one of the best in the world. Because Stefanie's case is so stubborn, it has often been the subject of brainstorming sessions among their top specialists. We've gotten great care. We're sure of that. It is one of the many privileges we enjoy.

But here's something else we know: the best doctors and the best medicine can't always fix you. Do you remember that grad student Stefanie was dating before she and I fell in love? His name is Bobby Willig. He became a professor of economics at Princeton, the chief economist in the Justice Department's Anti-Trust division, and the co-founder of the world's leading economics consulting firm. He and his wife, Ginny Mason, are the dearest friends we have. Their kids and grandkids are roughly the same ages as our kids and grandkids. All of them are great friends. Our families – each now three generations strong – hang out together every summer in Fourth Lake. When I did a couple of teaching gigs at Princeton, I stayed with them. When Bobby worked at Justice, he spent a lot of time with us. Many times over the years, the four of us have marveled at how smart we'd been to have paired up the way we did. Our seven children and 13 grandchildren agree. They all owe their lives to our clever choices. Funny how things work out.

In the fall of 2021, Bobby was diagnosed with an aggressive throat cancer that quickly migrated to his brain. Bobby, Ginny and their kids moved heaven and earth to get him the best treatment from the best doctors in the world. The docs threw everything they had at it. To no avail.

Bobby lived for another 13 months, most of them heartbreaking. Right from the start, he went into a physical and cognitive free-fall. We were never sure how much of this was the cancer and how much was the treatments. But we knew it was devastating. He lost 70 pounds; his limbs became sticks; his skin turned to parchment paper; he slept 20 hours a day, he moved around only with the help of a walker, a wheelchair or an aide. He never spoke above a whisper. He rarely strung together more than two or three coherent sentences. He thought months were days; morning was night. "Time for bed?" he'd ask after breakfast. His brilliant mind, gone. His acerbic wit, gone. His childlike whimsy, gone.

At least we assumed they were gone. We were never sure. One of his sons was convinced that behind that blank façade, Bobby was busy working out complex math equations to solve anti-trust cases. Another was sure his big personality was still there; it just couldn't get out of medical jail. We'd sometimes ask Bobby to help untangle the mystery. *Hey Bobby, do you understand stuff, but just can't communicate?*

Is that it? All we'd get back would be a sweet, passive smile – as if to say, *beats the hell of me.* Every now and then, there'd be a glimmer. At a big family gathering on Ginny's 73rd birthday he gave her a tender toast that left everyone in tears. Those moments were precious. But achingly rare.

Ginny's personality is as formidable as Bobby's. She's a social dynamo, a big-hearted friend, a loving matriarch. One of the hardest things she had to do during that miserable year was to figure out when to discontinue Bobby's treatments. It was clear from almost the outset that they weren't working – but hope springs eternal. It was also obvious that Bobby was in no condition to weigh in. Over the years the two of them talked about end-of-life. Bobby would sometimes quip that he wanted his head cryogenically frozen, a la Ted Williams, so he'd be around to take advantage of an as-yet-undiscovered miracle cure or Methuselah drug. That was a Bobby kind of joke (it *was* a joke, right?), but he was dead serious about wanting every possible medical intervention. Ginny, on the other hand, was firmly in the just-shoot-me camp. This created a dilemma for her. One of her doctors helped her resolve it. She told her: "Look, Ginny, he knew how you felt about end-of-life decisions. But he still made you his medical proxy. He trusted you to do the right thing." Ginny waited until everyone in the family was ready. By the time they decided, they were all at peace. Ginny was a tower of strength throughout.

Watching Bobby go that way – first losing his personhood, then his life – was the most gut-wrenching experience Stefanie and I have had with the death of a contemporary. Long before he died, Stefanie went into mourning. She found it excruciating to see him in that state. I too was deeply shaken. Several times during our many overnight visits that last year, I helped lift Bobby off the floor or helped clean him up. There's an intimacy to those encounters that's awkward and awful. And lovely. Alongside a half century of happier memories of Bobby in all his larger-than-life glory, those will not soon fade. I don't want them to.

Stefanie and I are closer than ever to Ginny and her kids. When we spend time now with her oldest son, we're startled by how much he reminds us of Bobby. Never noticed that before. Here's a passage from a Roger Angell essay that resonates:

"We geezers carry about a building directory of dead husbands or wives, children, parents, lovers, brothers and sisters, dentists, shrinks, office sidekicks, summer neighbors, classmates and bosses...It's no surprise we're a bit bent. The surprise, for me, is that the accruing weight of these departures doesn't bury us, and that even the pain of an almost unbearable loss gives way to something more distant but still stubbornly gleaming. The dead have departed but gestures and glances and tones of voice of theirs...reappear unexpectedly, along with accompanying touches of sweetness or irritation...Why do they sustain me so, cheer me up, remind me of life. I don't understand this. Why am I not endlessly grieving?"

I don't spend much time fretting about my death or Stefanie's, even though I'm familiar with the actuarial tables. That passage helps explain why. By the time you get to be our age, you've said goodbye to a lot of people you love. But you've also seen what they've left behind. They're gone, but not gone. A comforting thought.

Here's another: I don't know when we'll die, but I do know what will happen next. Stefanie and I will have our ashes spread onto the creek below our cabin, in the same spot where she and her siblings spread Norm and Bea's ashes.

That creek has been around for millions of years and will be around for millions more. It's left its mark on the place we love most in the world. Stefanie and I have left a mark there too. We, too, link past to future. Does this make us immortal? I think maybe it does.

CHAPTER ELEVEN

THE CAVALRY NEVER CAME

Fall, 2025

I kept waiting. Hoping. Pining.

Many times during the 2024 presidential campaign, I had a fever dream about the "aha moment" that would deliver America from its MAGA delusions.

One glorious day, millions of Trump supporters would snap to their senses, leap to their feet, stream onto the streets and shout out to their neighbors: "Damn, what I thinking?? This guy is fucking nuts!!"

I know that human nature doesn't work that way. No matter. I kept playing that fantasy tape in my brain because I desperately wanted it to be true. I teed it up whenever Trump went batshit crazy on the campaign trail – which, as you'll recall, was quite often. I played it when he said immigrants were vermin. When he called America a cesspool. When he sang the praises of the late, great Hannibal Lecter. When he hawked Trump Sneakers and Trump Bibles. When he claimed Haitians were eating the cats and dogs of Springfield, Ohio. When he admired Arnold Palmer's genitalia. When he obsessed over death by shark attack or electrocution. When he pretended to give his microphone a blow job. Each time, I thought to myself, "Yesss! We got him now."

But we didn't. For the second time in three elections, the villain prevailed. 2016 was a shock. This was far worse. This time around, America knew exactly what it was getting. This time, Trump won not despite the crassness, the cruelty, the chaos, the crazy, the bullshit, the lies. He won because of them.

Reading my campaign journal now, I'm reminded that interspersed among those flights of fantasy were stretches of dread. During the early months of 2024, it drove *me* crazy that his civil and criminal convictions hadn't put a dent in his approval ratings. On May 5, I wrote: "Damnit. Six months to go and he's still leading in the polls. This guy is the monster in a slasher movie. You cannot kill him."

My emotions ping-ponged for the rest of the campaign. In June, I was stunned (but not surprised) by Biden's disastrous debate performance. For more than a year, I'd been hoping, praying and – to the few stalwarts still willing to hear me out – loudly predicting that he wouldn't run for reelection. Now at this late date, after that performance, the fact that he *still* insisted on staying in the race struck me as the height of folly, vanity, self-delusion. I was beside myself.

A month later, when Biden grudgingly gave in to reality, I was elated. We have a chance!! We can rescue the values we hold most dear. We can break the MAGA fever. We can redeem America.

By the end of the Democratic convention in August. I was in full swoon over Kamala. I especially liked the closing passage of her acceptance speech, when she spoke of "the greatest privilege on Earth – the privilege and pride of being an American."

"Wow," I wrote in my journal, "The world turned upside down. In the Sixties my tribe was burning American flags. Now we're waving them, and the other guy is calling America a garbage can. We're gonna win!"

But the polls never budged. On Oct. 25 I wrote. "Panic! Hiding under my bed scared! Human nature – what a sonofabitch!"

A week later I was back to my sunny self. In those closing days, Trump had become the most unglued version of himself. This confirmed my theory of the case – at the end of the day, Donald Trump would defeat Donald Trump. Plus, I was heartened by the heavy turnout of women during the early voting period. "Looks like the cavalry has finally arrived!" I proclaimed on Nov. 2.

And that's how I saw the race right up until a few ticks after 8 p.m. on Nov. 5, when the first wave of county-level election returns started flashing onto our TV.   Instantly I could tell things were not unfolding as planned. I felt sick to my stomach. Beads of sweat formed on my forehead. I looked over at Stef. "We're fucked," I said. "We're fucked," she agreed.

I've never been so whipsawed – and so emotionally drained – by a political campaign. I saw 2024 as a morality play, a contest between good and evil. I wanted the villain to get his due. Much more important, I wanted the American people to deliver the verdict. Not a judge, not a jury. I wanted the entire country – guided by decency and virtue; fortified by facts and common sense –to put an end to Trump and Trumpism. I wanted Americans to redeem America.

But the cavalry never came. In 20/20 hindsight, the explanations seem painfully obvious. The porous border. The price of eggs. The smugness of elites. "Kamala is for they/them; President Trump is for you" (the anti-trans ad that saturated the airways). Trump himself may have had the sharpest post-election analysis. In his interview for Time Magazine's Person of the Year cover story, he called his campaign "72 days of fury," adding, "We hit the nerve of the country. The country was angry."

Trump is a maestro of grievance. "I am your warrior. I am your justice," he bellowed at rally after rally. "And for those who have been wronged and betrayed, I am your retribution."

This is his superpower. It's the only authentic thing about him. He's so adroit at triggering other people's grievances because he himself is so covetous, spiteful, resentful, needy. As J.D. Vance said of him: "He sees the worst in people, and he encourages the worst in people." (Vance said this in 2016). No matter whether in business or politics; in victory or defeat – Trump has spent all his life believing that the world is out to get him. It's an odd worldview for someone born to such privilege. But it's the deepest source of his bond with his followers. I'll leave it to others to decipher why Trump is the way he is.[36] I'd like to understand why his followers are the way they are.

One way to start is by widening the aperture beyond the issues that dominated the campaign. And for that matter, beyond America. Discontent has been brewing for decades in wealthy countries all over the world. Globalization, social media, and the knowledge economy have conspired to shrink the middle class, exacerbate income inequality, undermine institutions, breed distrust, foster loneliness, trigger grievance, weaken norms. It's a tough time for any politician to govern. In every developed country that held an election in 2024, the incumbent party lost vote share. This has never happened before. In most but not all cases, voters punished parties of the center/left, which typically promote activist government policies. Biden left office with his approval/disapproval rating underwater at 37%-55%, but he was a paragon of popularity compared with Canada's Trudeau

---

[36]   *Trump's niece, psychologist Mary L. Trump, has written two books describing the toxic brew of abuse, neglect and gratuitous cruelty that permeated the home of her grandparents, Fred and Mary Trump, where she lived for much of her childhood. The elder Trumps produced two sons. One (Mary's father) drank himself to death at 42. The other became president of the United States.*

(26%-68%), Germany's Shultz (19%-75%) and France's Macron (18%-75%).

Trump rode that global wave of discontent. Even though he carried the popular vote by a mere 1.5 percentage points, the rightward shift of America's electorate was breathtaking in its breadth. Between 2020 and 2024, more than 90 percent of the nation's counties swung toward the GOP.

He made his greatest gains among the young, among the working class and poor, and among non-whites, especially non-white men. Two statistical trends tell the tale. In 2012, Obama carried the non-white working class by 67 percentage points; in 2024, Harris carried those voters by just 32 percentage points. And in 2024, for the first time in modern history, Democrats did better with the richest third of the electorate than with the poorest third.

Class, not race, was the decisive demographic drama of the 2024 election. But now comes an irony. To the extent that rich and poor shifted their political allegiances, each group swung against economic self-interest. The wealthy warmed to Harris, despite the fact that she vowed to raise their taxes; the poor and working class warmed to Trump, despite the fact that he barely bothered to hide his intention to shrink their safety net. In both cases, their votes were driven at least as much by the culture as by the economy. Well-off Americans are comfortable with the new America and all its trappings. The diverse, multi-cultural, knowledge economy has been good to them. The less well-off feel aggrieved, cheated, forsaken, downwardly mobile.

Burn-the-house-down populism carried the day. We'll see how far Trump 47 gets with his blowtorch. Any coalition that marries the interests of billionaire tech broligarchs with those of working-class stiffs seems bound for grief. Trump has been riding high for most of his first year,[37] but it's early days yet. We'll see. For those who fear that we're in for a long spell of right-wing authoritarianism, here are some numbers that may calm your nerves. In each of the last three presidential elections, the incumbent party has been kicked out of the White House. This hadn't happened in 120 years. In the past two decades, partisan control of the White House, the House and the Senate have all changed hands four times. This had never happened before. In the past ten presidential elections (which split 5-5 between Ds and Rs), the margin of victory has always been in single digits. This too had never happened before.

Twenty-first century America is a nation deeply but evenly divided. Neither party has come up with an enduring response to our pervasive discontent. There are no long-term partisan majority coalitions on the horizon, as there had been in the eras of FDR and Ronald Reagan. The tables, having turned, are likely to keep turning. One day the backlash will have a backlash. The only question is when – and after how much damage.

As for me, a reckoning is at hand right now. How did I miss all this? How did I get so stupid? Not a pleasant line of inquiry at any stage of life; especially fraught in old age, when the likelihood of re-mediation is vanishingly small. But hey, might as well go there. Here are some things that 2024 taught me about me.

I'm good at seeing how other people can get stuck in their echo chambers. I'm no good at seeing how I can get stuck in mine.[38] Do I suffer from Trump Derangement Syndrome? Yup. But am I right? Yup.

---

[37] *"I have a right to do anything I want to – I'm the president of the United States!!" Trump proclaimed at televised cabinet meetings that consisted of one appointee after another lavishing his majesty with adulation.*

[38] *In the summer of 2024, my son Jeremy suggested I take a break from my diet of liberal pundits and spend some time listening to Joe Rogan's podcast. "Who is Joe Rogan?" I responded.*

I think of Americans as expert bullshit detectors, but I've overestimated their aversion to it. In the case of Trump, they saw it for what it was. And gave it a pass. People have a hard time admitting they've been conned. It's easier to double down.

I thought the big question of 2024 wasn't whether America could be great (it's always been great), but whether it could be good. I cared about that a lot. I overestimated how much others did.

I'm good at documenting the many changes that have been roiling America in this new century – new immigrants, new cultures, new technologies, new racial groups, new gender identities, new sexual affinities. But I've overestimated the upside of change; underestimated the backlash.

I also overestimated Americans' basic command of reality. In retrospect, I should have paid more attention to surveys that show more than a third of Americans think the 2020 election was stolen from Trump and a quarter believe the January 6 rioters were victims of an FBI trap. And to a 2022 YouGov survey that asked Americans to estimate what share of our population is made up of various groups. The responses take one's breath away: Transsexuals, 21%; Muslims, 27%; Jews, 30%; Blacks, 41%. (The actual figures: 1%, 1%, 2% and 12%). Clearly, lots of Americans confuse their fears and fantasies with facts.

In my patriotic (and chauvinistic) love for my country, I've been slow to face up to some evident character flaws. The line that most gnawed at me after Trump's 2016 election came from author Kurt Andersen: "America has always been a land of hucksters and their suckers." In the same vein, historian Stephen Kotkin wrote after the 2024 election that Trump "reflects something deep and abiding about American culture. Think of all the worlds that he has inhabited and that lifted him up. Pro wrestling. Reality TV. Casinos and gambling… Celebrity culture. Social media. All of that looks to me like America. And yes, so does fraud, and brazen lying, and the P.T. Barnum, carnival barker stuff. But there is an audience, and not a small one, for where Trump came from and who he is."

I paid too little attention to the power of the dark web. Humans have always been animated by conspiracy theorists and hate mongers, but the internet is a force multiplier. On the web, crazy can find crazy. And social media rage entrepreneurs – motived by ideology or greed or both– can market hate as click bait and spread it like a contagion.

I've always considered myself an idealist without illusions. Apparently I'm an idealist *with* illusions. Some of you may wonder, well, am I just flattering myself? Too good and pure for this cruel world? That's my sad discovery in old age?

But no, this is a painful reckoning. The people I admire most in public life are those who see the world as it really is but still hang on to their humanity as they try to make things better. I fancied myself someone who could improve politics and public life by making sure voters got the best possible information during election campaigns. But if I never understood that voters sometimes – often? –make choices that have little to do with facts, reason or enlightened self-interest, did I ever have a chance of making things better?

I don't know the answer. I don't like the question. Here's another question I can't answer: If I were still a newspaper reporter, how would I do my job in the Trump Era? Would I make some effort to see the world through eyes of his MAGA faithful? Or would I spend my energy showing how detached they are from (my understanding of) reality?

If the former, there's a passage from sociologist Arlie Hochschild that I'd like to think would inform my coverage: "If you're a Trump voter, here's your deep story: You're waiting in a long line leading up to the American Dream. The line is not moving…Then you see people you perceive as "line cutters": women, Black and brown people, immigrants, refugees, and well-paid public servants. You notice a bad bully in line who is helping these undeserving line-cutters. But — hey — there is the good bully, who is going to help people like you. Yes, he has flaws, but he is still your bully: Donald Trump."

Could I summon that level of empathy for Trump supporters? Those are the instincts I brought to the job when I was a reporter. But it was easier then. I wrote about conflicts between parties or races or interest groups or social classes or ideological camps. My sympathies were often with one side (typically the underdog), but my job – which I took very seriously – was to keep those feelings in check as I reported on all sides from multiple perspectives.

For a journalist, there's another reason to observe the world from many angles – economic self-interest. When the public sees us taking sides, we lose our best claim to their attention and their subscription fees – our credibility. We become just another blogger, influencer, TikToker. One more angry voice in the digital Tower of Babel.

And yet. And yet. In Trump's world, the conflicts are not merely between red and blue. They're between truth and lies, information and disinformation, democracy and autocracy. Hard to be even-handed about that. If you give his reign of vengeance and lawlessness the attention it commands, if you call him out for his flamboyant lies and pathetic boasts, his lust for dominance, his grandiosity, his cruelty, his grift and graft, you risk becoming an opposition press. If you don't, you risk becoming a propaganda arm of the state. There's barely a middle ground. I don't envy the editors and reporters in today's newsrooms. It goes against their instincts, interests, values and temperament to take sides. But they have no choice. Their most important job is to speak truth to power. If they can pull that off and at the same time shed an empathetic light on the sources of Trump's populist appeal, they'll have thread the needle and done honor to their calling.

I also know this: My revulsion for Trump is personal. He's a weakling and a thug. He trashes the values I hold dear. He's exposed aspects of the American character that drive me to despair. When he says the news is fake, he doesn't just want people to disbelieve stories about him. He wants them to believe that truth itself is irrelevant because everything is rigged. Many of his followers believe him.

Early in Trump's second term, David Brooks captured my feelings of moral shame: "If there is an underlying philosophy driving Trump, it is this: Morality is for suckers. The strong do what they want and the weak suffer what they must. This is the logic of bullies everywhere. Day after day, the administration works to create a world where ruthless people can thrive. The truth itself is a restraint on power, so it must be abandoned. Lying becomes the language of the state."

April, 2026. For sanity's sake, I'd resolved a year ago to limit my exposure to the torrent of news about Trump 2.0. This hasn't worked out. As his march toward authoritarianism has become more ominous, I've become the rubbernecker who covers his eyes only to peek – then stare – through parted fingers.

Masked ICE thugs murdering civilians in Minneapolis. Naval bombardiers murdering suspected drug runners in the Caribbean. The kow-towing to Putin. The trolling of Canada, the Fed, the Supreme Court. The designs on Greenland. The reckless war on Iran. The propaganda videos that portrayed it as a video game. The profanity-laced threat to obliterate an entire civilization. The neutering of Congress. The bulldozing of the White House. The billion-dollar side hustles of Trump's family and friends. Trump's name on the Kennedy Center, his signature on the currency, his face on a gold coin, his banner above the entrance to the Justice Department.

And he keeps getting crazier. Last October, after a nationwide No Kings protest, he posted an AI-generated video of himself wearing a crown and piloting a fighter jet that dumped feces on the protestors below. In February, he posted another video that portrayed Michelle and Barack Obama as apes.[39] To many (but not all) of his MAGA fans, this was Trump "owning the libs" and "Trump being Trump." Good fun! Nothing to see here! I like political satire as much as the next guy, but what I saw was late-stage narcissistic personality disorder, early-stage dementia and unvarnished racism. Maybe you saw something similar.

Before the 2024 election, I'd hoped that Trump would wind up as an historical footnote, his political epitaph drawn from George W. Bush's critique of his "American carnage" inaugural address in 2017: "That was some weird shit." But alas, Trump is destined to go down in history as an era, not an aberration. To add insult to injury, he's exposed me as a fool.

And a fool I remain. Despite everything, Trump has not beaten the Pollyanna out of me. I despise what is happening in his America. I'm despondent at how many pillars of the establishment have bent the knee. I'm depressed by the ugliness in our public square. But I believe this too will pass. Our constitution is too resilient. Our multi-culturalism is too ingrained. Our public is too pragmatic. Our society is too dynamic. Trump is too old and too nuts. One day, the clouds will lift, and America will be good again. Adam Smith wrote that in every nation, "there is a great deal of ruin." Surely that's true of America. But we've endured for 250 years. Along the way, we've survived slavery, the Trail of Tears, the Civil War, the Know Nothings; Jim Crow; the Ku Klux Klan, the Palmer Raids, the Red Scare, communism, fascism. We will survive Donald Trump.

One Day, Everyone Will Have Always Been Against This won the 2025 National Book Award for non-fiction.[40] The book isn't about Trump

---

[39] *The blowback was so overwhelming that the White House pulled the post down the day it appeared. Trump claimed he never saw the offensive image, blamed a staffer and declined to apologize.*

[40] *Egyptian-born author Omar El Akkad's book is a critique of Western imperialism that focuses on the war in Gaza.*

but its title captures my hopes for tomorrow's America. Since I've stopped pretending to be a seer, I offer this thought neither as a prediction nor an expression of optimism. It's an assertion of faith. Everyone should have faith in something. I have faith in my country. Still.

Indeed, I've never felt so patriotic, in part because loving America has never taken so much effort. "To be a patriot in Donald Trump's America is like sitting through a loved one's trial for some gruesome crime." George Packer wrote in The Atlantic. "Day after day your shame deepens as the horrifying testimony piles up, until you wonder how you can still care about this person….And yet you keep showing up, exchanging smiles and waves, hoping for some mitigating evidence to emerge – trying to believe in your country's essential decency."

I believe in the decency I found on the other side of those screen doors when I was a political reporter. That Stefanie and I encountered as we traded banter with tradespeople during our renovation project. That I saw on television in streets of Minneapolis this year as everyday Americans banded together to protect their immigrant neighbors from Trump's thugs.

America is the only country in the world whose culture, creed and very existence originate from an idea — that we're all created equal. We've never fully made good on that idea. But it's still the best idea anyone's ever had for a country. Now more than ever, it's worth celebrating, defending. preserving, perfecting.

CHAPTER TWELVE

INKY'S BABIES' ROAD TO HELL

Fall, 2025

In the fall of 1966, a thousand young men converged on New Haven as members of the most revolutionary freshman class ever admitted to Yale. We were chosen to advance three goals. Modernize Yale. Democratize America. Save the world.

Impossibly grandiose? Well, duh. But these were the Sixties, this was Yale, we were the Baby Boomers, everything was possible.

This past spring a couple hundred of us returned for our 55th reunion. Along with creaky knees and extra pounds, many – myself included – carried a backpack of regrets about the way the road to hell can be paved with good intentions.

Politically, boomers are a mish-mash. Most are conservative, but most boomer elites – like my Yale classmates and me – are liberal. Elites set the table for the culture, which sets the table for the politics. Here's where the lifetime report card for the Yale Class of 1970 and others of our persuasion gets uncomfortable.

Back in the Sixties we helped lead the fights for civil rights and personal freedoms. Thanks at least in part to our idealism and activism, today's America is a vastly better place for women, minorities, gays, immigrants, the disabled.

But there's a disturbing through-line between yesterday's social justice crusades and today's political and civic dystopia. The anti-establishment passions that fueled us then have been turned against us now – weaponized by Trump to dismantle the policies and programs we hold most dear.

No doubt some of this backlash was inevitable. History moves in cycles; human beings don't adapt easily to change. You invent the ship, you invent the shipwreck. But in 20/20 hindsight, much of today's hellscape might have been avoided, or at least mitigated. It turns out we boomer elites made a lot of mistakes.

- We paid too little attention to the way that immigration, globalization, pluralism and the knowledge economy did wonders for us but stunted the economic prospects and "stole the pride" (to use Arlie Russell Hochschild's phrase) of the working class. They resent our neglect, our lip service, our condescension. This has given Trump his fuel. He too hates elites. And he has a feral genius for exploiting grievance.
- We misjudged the importance of institutions. We saw them as instruments of oppression, as they surely can be. But they are also indispensable guardians of a nation's values. After we won our victories, we should have worked to restore the public trust that we'd helped to undermine. This has come back to bite us. Back then, we thought America's institutions were rigged. Now, that's exactly how MAGA feels.
- We got lost in our own echo chamber. On our watch, elite universities like Yale became ground zero for the progressive mindset. But they've drifted away from the rest of America. In the 2024 election cycle, 97% of the campaign contributions

made by Yale faculty and employes went to Democrats. Does that sound like a campus where a range of views can be debated in the best tradition of intellectual inquiry? Many other bastions of the establishment, anchors of civil society and keepers of the culture – legacy media, Hollywood, Madison Avenue, foundations, non-profits, the arts community, swaths of corporate America – have gone down similar rabbit holes. It helps that we happen to be right about just about everything. But I get nervous whenever I remember a quote from John Stuart Mill I first encountered as a Yale freshman: "He who knows only his side of the case knows little of that."

- We've waged an undeclared war on tomorrow's America. This has been a bipartisan boomer travesty – and no, this isn't a story of good intentions gone awry. Decade after decade, the liberals and conservatives we've sent to Washington DC have knowingly enacted policies that have made boomers richer and future Americans poorer. Our grandkids will spend their lives paying off the federal debt we've racked up. A decade from now, Social Security and Medicare will be insolvent. The fixes will be painful – benefit cuts, tax increases, both. But by then, tens of millions of us boomers will have collected full benefits and gone on to our greater rewards, unscathed. OK Boomer!

- We never figured out the art of bipartisan compromise. The last time America took a stab at fixing Social Security's long-term demographic problems was in 1983. Our last stab at comprehensive immigration reform came in 1987. Both of those bipartisan bills were forged by leaders from older generations. Boomers have fired blanks each time we aimed for solutions of that scope and nature – not just for those persistent challenges, but for others like climate change and gun violence.

In preparation for our 55th reunion, my classmate Jim Conroy and I took a survey of our class. The results were striking. By our own reckoning, our lives have turned out great. We're happy with our families, proud of our careers, secure in our finances (our median net wealth is roughly $3 million), and optimistic about our remaining years.

But we're in a deep funk about our country. Asked if the United States will still be a constitutional democracy a decade from now, 43% said they're pessimistic, just 24% said they're optimistic; the remaining third are unsure. Asked if political turbulence today is more worrisome than it was during our college years – with its deadly urban riots, political assassinations and antiwar protests – 77% said things are worse now; just 3% said things were worse then.

Some of their comments:

- "Then the disruption was coming from us. Now it's coming from a malign collection of wannabe authoritarians."
- "Difference between then and now is, of course, that no matter how demented politicians were in the 1960s, 1970s, etc., none of them were rampaging all-out to end democracy."
- "Why is everything so cruel?"
- "Off the charts in this moment. F'ing ridiculous."

Just 10% of our respondents identified as conservative. Here's what one had to say.

- "Lefties, you need to dial it back. You keep taking laudable, commendable principles and diving way off the deep end with them, alienating some centrist voters like me [and] gift-wrapping the White House back to that Satan traitor for a second term."

The Yale Class of 1970 did not come to these world views by accident. We were an experiment in social and academic engineering directed by a blue blood Republican whose ancestors arrived on the Mayflower.

When Kingman Brewster, Jr. became its president in 1963, Yale was still admitting most of its students from exclusive prep schools, with a special fondness for the sons of wealthy Yale alumni.[41]

Brewster himself came from old money and had attended a prep school. But he could see that the world was changing and the marketplace of knowledge was exploding. "I do not intend to preside over a finishing school on the Long Island Sound," he told a colleague. He wanted to educate a new generation of Yale men who would "break new ground or at least adapt to it"; men who could solidify America's place as the leader of the free world. He said he hoped the next generation's Martin Luther King would be a Yale graduate.

The Class of 1970 was the first recruited by Brewster's handpicked Director of Admissions, R. Inslee Clark, Jr. – he too a prep school product. Clark sent his staff around the country to public schools that had never before seen a Yale recruiter. A record 58% of my freshman class were public high school graduates. The share of Jews, no longer suppressed by Yale's unofficial quota, shot up to a record 30%. The share of racial minorities was still in single digits but no longer miniscule. Our median verbal SAT score was 697, best in Yale's history (and better than Harvard's!). We were dubbed "Inky's Babies."

The faculty was thrilled, but Brewster took flak from the alumni, who saw him as a traitor to his class. "You will laugh," wrote an exasperated William F. Buckley Jr., Yale's most famous alumnus of that era, "but a Mexican-American from El Paso High with identical scores on the achievement test, and identically ardent recommendations from

---

[41] For an excellent overview of Brewster's stewardship of Yale, see a biography by Geoffrey Kabaservice, *The Guardians: Kingman Brewster, His Circle, and the Rise of the Liberal Establishment.* New York: Henry Holt and Company, 2004.

the headmaster, has a better chance of being admitted to Yale than Jonathan Edwards the Sixteenth from Saint Paul's School."

Brewster was undeterred. In quick succession, Yale adopted a needs-blind admissions policy and did away with its coat-and-tie rule, its numerical grading system and its prohibition on women visiting men in their dorm rooms at night. The biggest and best break from tradition came in 1969, when, for the first time in 268 years, Yale opened its ivy gates to female undergraduates.

All the while, Inky's Babies did our thing. Civil rights demonstrations. Anti-war protests. Draft-dodging schemes. Summer of Love. Woodstock. Sex, drugs, and rock n roll. When our campus activism threatened to turn violent in the spring of 1970, Brewster kept the peace by suspending "normal academic expectations" for the remainder of the term. I graduated a few weeks later without writing my last papers or taking my final exams.

Much of America no doubt saw us as a bunch of pampered flower children, but could also tell we were a force to be reckoned with – witness that Time Magazine Person of the Year trophy bestowed on us in 1967. We've been a supremely self-assured generation ever since. We've taken good care of ourselves. But look what we've done to the young.

This is the most damning indictment of the boomer era. Our kids and grandkids are not doing well. Their malaise goes way beyond politics and economics. America's young adults rank 62nd in the world in self-reported life satisfaction, according to the latest findings from the World Happiness Report. They are wary about making friends, finding romance, getting married, having kids. Back when the boomer generation was conceived (1946-1964), America's total fertility rate was 3.0 children per woman. Now it's 1.6. The share of adults who are married was 75% then. It's 50% now. These are not markers of a society that feels good about itself or hopeful about the future.

One of the best parts of a Yale reunion is the chance to sit in on lectures by faculty superstars and find out what they're teaching the next generation of America's elites. I attended three, each of them fascinating.

Laurie Santos gave us a souped-up version of The Science of Happiness, which has been the most popular course at Yale for the past decade. She opened with grim statistics about the mental health of today's youth: 40% say there are days when they're too depressed to function; 10% say they have seriously considered suicide. These trends have been building for many years. Santos cited a familiar litany of causes – the ill effects of social media and the pandemic; the rise of income inequality; the "dumpster fire" of our civic and political culture; anxiety about climate change and school shootings.

Her remedies were familiar too: seek out more human connections; say nice things to other people; make time for gratitude; savor the good things; focus on your strengths; get more sleep; give yourself the gift of self-compassion. Not exactly rocket science, but revelatory. Apparently this is what tomorrow's leaders need to hear.

Amy Chua is known both as the author of *The Battle Hymn of the Tiger Mom* and as a mentor to one of her Yale Law students, J.D. Vance. She's also written a book about tribalism, a condition she described as hard-wired in human biology. "Studies show that our brains light up when we stick it to the other side."

But as Chua tells it, there's very little of that happening in Yale classrooms, where students hold their tongues out of fear of the cancel culture. "Sometimes they will email me their honest views privately." Outside the classroom, Chua said, students self-segregate by race and ethnicity and don't dare strike up friendships or romances across political boundaries.

I'm guessing other Yale faculty might take issue with the starkness of her portrait, but I doubt many would disagree with her remedies. Chua wants America to create a national service program where young adults from all walks of life would have to interact with one another. She also called for a new national commitment to a civics curriculum that tells hard truths about America's flaws "while still conveying the idea that we are a great nation." "We've overcorrected," she said. "Too many of our students think of the founding fathers as dead white male racists."

Akhil Amar, Yale's great constitutional scholar, made a similar argument. "America needs a new national narrative because we don't have one," he told a standing-room-only auditorium. He suggested we build it around the constitution, which he extolled as "the only thing that makes us a we." He vented his outrage at the way Trump and his lawyers keep trying to torch it. "We're living in a golden age of lying," he said. "They just make shit up."

~

Most of my Yale '70 classmates are, like Amar, astonished and infuriated by the gusher of bullshit, chaos and cruelty erupting each day from Trump's White House. In our class reunion survey, more than a third said they've become more spiritual – partly because age has sanded off their sharp edges; partly because they need a way to cope with the political hellscape. Several spoke of using daily meditation sessions to stay grounded.

Others are staying in the fight. Charles Thomas, 77, is an Assistant U.S. Attorney for the Western District of Missouri whose portfolio includes enforcing the rights of disabled people. "As appealing as some aspects of my work are, I feel a need to start a new phase of my life," he told me. "I want to be more fully involved and enmeshed with the poor and the oppressed."

In early 2025 Charles applied to serve in the Peace Corps. He was initially accepted, but when he subsequently had to have a stent placed in his right coronary artery, he was rejected on medical grounds. This would have been Charles' second Peace Corps tour. Shortly after graduating from Yale, he did his first stint as a public health worker combating tuberculosis in rural South Korea. "As a 12 year old I had listened to President Kennedy giving the speech that called for the creation of the Peace Corps. He appealed to America's idealism. From that moment on, I knew I wanted to be a Peace Corps volunteer."

Charles is still looking for ways to serve. In February 2026, he emailed me: "I am thinking about seeking a job teaching high school in inner-city Kansas City. I'm also looking into international volunteer opportunities with the American Friends Service Committee, the United Nations, or other organizations. I would love to work in the Rohingya refugee camp in Bangladesh, or in Gaza."

Charles may be in a class by himself, but lots of members of our Class of 1970 are still doing public-spirited work deep into their seventies – in medical practices, research labs, law firms, classrooms, advocacy and civic groups, news organizations. Inky's Babies became admirable men – and admirable old men. I think Kingman Brewster would be proud of us.

However, our generation never produced the next JFK or MLK. Nor did we do enough to protect the values, norms and institutions that truly make America great. When the center doesn't hold; when the rich get richer and the middle hollows out, demagogues can rush in to fill the void. That's one lesson we never heeded.

Other lessons we've learned well. Our survey invited my classmates to reflect on the best and worst things about getting old. And we asked what advice about aging they'd give to younger folks. As their responses attest, we're all quite different. And pretty much the same.

Worst

- Failing to watch my weight. Pontificating.

- Accepting that I can no longer run or swim long distances.
- Controlling my impatience with others.
- Dealing with repurposing my professional interests in the absence of work and the structure it provides.
- Hair on my ears.
- I keep trying to improve my 5K times instead of cruising into a leisurely pace. And I'm failing at improving my times!
- Letting go of lust.
- I worry too much about people seeing me as old.
- Not thinking I am 19 years old.
- Ruminating too much about the past, and how some things could have been different.
- I've gone through life pretty self-satisfied. As I get closer to the end, however, I realize I have consistently self-aggrandized.
- Regret – worked too much at the expense of my children.
- The time it takes to get going in the morning.
- Things that I have zero control over. Hearing loss and sexual performance top the list.
- Tracking days & dates. And those pesky names.
- Tying my shoes.

Best

- Listening more, talking less. Deferring to children and watching grandchildren.
- More patient with myself, and with life.
- My grammar is still quite good.
- Pride in how well my children are doing in life, and how they feel about me.
- Having spent my career caring for children, I find I am getting better at talking with older people.
- I don't beat myself up over taking naps.
- Walking more slowly.

- Working hard to tie up loose ends.
- Managing money so it doesn't run out before my wife or I do.
- I am grateful for the life I have lived as I have tried to give back through a career in education and in seeking justice.
- From this vantage point, I can now appreciate how rich and smooth the road has been, though I didn't always know it at the time.

Advice

- Don't blink. Your two-year old will be 18 when you get up tomorrow. At 45 you can't imagine how fast the next 35 years will go. Stay physically active!
- Don't let anything stop you; keep on fighting for what you believe in.
- Enjoy and savor slowing down. Be grateful every day and cherish those you love. "The joy in life is life itself."
- Fear not. Insist on freedom and being happy. Stay kind to others and yourself. Limit regrets.
- Nothing is ever as good or bad as it seems at first.
- Say "yes" a lot.
- Shower the people you love with love.
- You don't stop laughing when you grow old; you grow old when you stop laughing.
- The adage with age comes wisdom is false. I see no empirical support for that proposition.
- No one gets out of this alive.
- As you get old time goes faster and faster – it never slows down.
- Don't hold grudges. Forgiveness for all.
- Don't worry about that ache or pain; something different will hurt tomorrow!
- Find God or he might just have to find you.
- Balance is more important than success.

- "It takes one a long time to become young" – Picasso.
- "I've mastered not philosophy…and here I stand, with all my hard and studied lore. A poor misguided fool, no wiser than I was before."
- I worked hard to do well in my career, and mostly I did. But now what was accomplished has somewhat faded, and I realize that it is the people I met along the way, and how I could help others, that matters more.
- Younger self – don't smoke tobacco.
- There's no silver bullet for a good life. Everyone's different. Most people are pretty messed up, so if you're not, it was a good life. Enjoy it and pass it on to others.
- Trying to figure out what consciousness is all about is impossible, and yet it's the most fun thing about "being here." Meditation 60 years so far, and I've gotten a few inches toward a shred of understanding.
- You may be the last person you get to know but keep trying.

There you have it: trinkets and pearls from a bunch of old Yalies, loosely strung together around a few basic ideas about old age. Accept. Adapt. Adjust. Be grateful.

Wise advice for our generation at dusk. Not much help for younger generations as they grapple with the mess we've left behind. For 250 years, Americans have been taught to expect that life always gets better. The Declaration of Independence enshrines "the pursuit of happiness" as a God-given right, entitled to government protection. No nation in history had ever dreamt of making such an audacious guarantee. The boomers' expectations were especially grand, reflecting the triumphalism of our birth years. But societies, economies and politicians can't always make good on the promise of perpetual upward mobility. When progress falls short, dark impulses take root. Trump and MAGA have spun them into political gold.

However, they don't have the last word. In America, no political movement does. It will be up to the progressive left in younger generations to resist, then repair. A tall order, not an impossible one. In our remaining years, we boomers should give them all the support we can muster. From the sidelines. Surely we owe them that.

CHAPTER THIRTEEN

GROWING OLD IN FOURTH LAKE

Summer, 2025

For the longest time I thought we'd never finish the renovation. I was mistaken. Yes, a few major improvements still await – new heating system, new foam insulation underneath the house, new landscaping. And yes, the parade of minor projects will never cease. Among the fixes of the past year: door knobs, switch plates, lighting, shelving. But Stefanie and I have crossed a psychological Rubicon. We're no longer renovating our vacation house. We're just living in it.

And here's the best part: In harmony.

The marital wounds of the construction years have mostly healed. Miraculously, we've reached a ceasefire in the War of the Rocks. This was Stef's doing. Her counterintuitive terms: More rocks. Those boulders she never wanted alongside the new stairs are now attached to a wall of smaller rocks that extends to the far side of the old stairway, thirty feet away. The rocks somehow soften the boulders, which was Stef's goal. And the wall forms a symmetrical frame around the slope in front of the house, where we've planted flowering bushes, native grasses and ferns, creating a woodsy look that complements the waterfall.

The front stairs.

The waterfall.

The house in fall.

Is there a more sublime satisfaction in life than figuring out how to do something difficult, then doing it, then seeing that it turned out well? That's how Stef and I feel about our five-year odyssey. When we sit down for breakfast, we often take a moment to marvel at all the interior spaces we've transformed.[42] Stefanie sometimes fantasizes about how Norm and Bea would react if they could see the place

---

[42] *I do the same thing whenever I sit on the toilet. The master bedroom bathroom renovation was a beast. Non-stop troubles with the new shower, the new bathtub, the new countertop, the new underfloor heating, the new lighting, the new wainscotting, the new baseboards, the new trim — and, most of all, the new plumber, who walked out mid-job, probably high on drugs. But between Stef's tiling, my carpentry, and our non-stop improvising, we overcame. And now, whenever I sit on the pot, I admire. Hundred problems, hundred solutions.*

now. "Daddy would be going from room to room saying, 'Wow! Wow! Wow! Holy shit!!' And mom would be saying: : 'Norman! How much do you think this costs? Norman, how much do you think that costs'?[43] But she'd love it too."

The more we worked on the house, the more we came to understand how much this project was about them. We've hung a bunch of their pictures on the family photo wall, including two World War II era classics – Norm in his Army uniform, smoking a cigarette; Bea looking glamorous in the photo she sent him when he was stationed in post-war Germany, helping to de-Nazify towns and villages. Alongside these photos, there's a framed local newspaper article that chronicled their own audacious do-it-yourself construction adventure in 1974. And near that, we've hung the hand-painted "Casa Teitel" nameplate that used to adorn the front door.

Norm and Bea built the house for themselves and their kids. We've rebuilt it for ourselves and our kids. One day, if the stars and moons align, they'll do the same for themselves and their kids. That's why the project has cast such a spell. It links us to our past and to our future. It has made Norm and Bea immortal. One day we hope it will do that for us too.

I'm pretty sure all Fourth Lakers have similar feelings – if not about a particular house, then about the community itself. We're a collection of three, four and five generation families. Each summer we reconvene to revisit our youth, remember our parents, raise our children, reconnect with our friends, commune with nature. As the years go by, the roots grow deeper, the generational threads thicker, the urge to leave a legacy stronger.

Our 50 families own a total of 62 houses here. Making room for successive generations, each larger than its predecessor, is a high-class problem, but a problem nonetheless. You have to navigate the

---

[43]   *Here's the good news, Bea and Norm: We've saved a small fortune by doing it ourselves. Just the way you taught us.*

math, the real estate, the finances, the family dynamics. A further complication: the community association has a cap on memberships (60, with exceptions for lineal descendants) along with a geographic boundary on housing lots (they must be located within walking distance of the lake). Typically, the adult offspring with the deepest attachment to the community inherits the family house. Sometimes siblings share ownership. Or, if they can, they'll buy or build a house of their own. Or they'll just visit. Or they'll drift away. Usually all this gets worked out amicably. But families are family; things can get ugly. Some siblings haven't seen or spoken to each other for decades. And sometimes, entire families up and leave. Maybe the social life wasn't working for them, or their kids didn't like it here, or there's been a death, a divorce, a financial or health setback. When they put their house on the market, their buyers are often the families that need to make room for their expanding broods. And so we're propelled forward by a benign form of natural selection: Survival of the happiest.

Over the years there have been two Fourth Lake intermarriages, both involving a Teitel. Fifty years ago Stef's brother Lee married Laura, a childhood buddy of all of ours. Their wedding was in the then-newly-built living room of what's now our house. For the past 30 years they've had their own house, built by Lee, that sits about a hundred and fifty yards west of ours. Last year Stef's sister Beth and her husband Bill[44] sold their New Jersey house and built a year-round house here. It sits halfway between Lee's house and ours, and replaces the summer house that they'd been living in for the past 30 years. Another hundred and fifty yards farther west sits the house where I spent my summers as a kid before inheriting it from my parents, who had inherited it from my grandparents. It's where Stef and I raised our kids in the summers. Now it's where our daughter and her family

---

[44]   *In Teitel family nomenclature, Beth "married out" because her husband Bill didn't spend his childhood summers here. After 40-plus years, his probationary period is almost done.*

spend their summers. When our sons and their families visit, which is often, they usually stay with Stef and me in the "creek house." Most nights we all assemble for a big family dinner around the big white oak table that James built, in the room that he and I built, for a meal that Stefanie prepared. After dinner, the cousins all romp, the older ones doting on the younger ones, while their parents try not very hard to keep a lid on the chaos and grandma and grandpa quietly collapse. Can life possibly get any better?

Living under the same roof with your grandchildren is "like seeing the world in shades of gray, with your eyesight dimmed by hard experience, and then suddenly the gray is gone," New York Times columnist David French wrote about the joys of co-habiting with his grandkids during Covid. "All the bright colors explode back into your life."

For Stefanie and me, life in Fourth Lake is feast or famine. All chaos all the time when the kids and grandkids are around. Peaceful, serene, and deliciously dull when they're not. We love both seasons – so much so that our summers in Fourth Lake now stretch from late May through early January. We adopted that schedule to accommodate the construction project. But it turns out we stumbled onto a pretty perfect setting for an even more daunting challenge: Old age.

The creek in winter

Best place in the world

Our deck is a tree house

Gerontologists point to the same three factors that predict a happy, healthy and long life – good diet, regular exercise, positive attitude. Then there's a fourth that appears to be most powerful of all: strong relationships.

That's the famous finding of the most extensive longitudinal study of human happiness ever done, the Harvard Study of Adult Development. It began tracking 268 Harvard students in 1938 and followed them and subsequent cohorts over the full arc of their lives.[45] It found that, when all other factors are held constant, having close relationships has been the strongest single predictor of happiness and longevity among the Harvard men.

---

[45]   *Among the early participants: John F. Kennedy and Ben Bradlee.*

Relationships can come in any variety – spouse, child, sibling, partner, co-worker, neighbor, friend. The older we get, the harder they are to maintain but the more important they become. The study shows that they're the sturdiest line of defense against the old-age demons of loneliness, isolation, boredom, irrelevance, depression, despair. To which Stefanie and I would add: If you can pull it off, grow old with old friends, which is what we're doing in Fourth Lake. They knew you way back when; they know you now; they know how you got from there to here. You know them the same way. We've all had different joys and sorrows, of course. But we've all taken our journeys at the same time and in the same place. And now, as we approach the horizon, we all have similar ghosts and memories. Here are some of mine:

It is 1959. I am 10 years old. I'm sitting on the beach, watching a group of teenagers play volleyball. One of the girls, maybe 16 or 17, has a lovely figure. I am just old enough to notice. She is wearing a halter top and, as I would discover, no bra. At one point, as she reaches up with both hands to make a shot, her halter rises up. From my vantage point seated on the sand, I see her breasts. In my entire young life, I had never encountered anything so astonishing.

It is 1960. I am 11 years old. I've just lost a set of tennis to my mom, and I'm throwing a fit. Tennis is a big deal in our family. My dad and brother are tournament-level amateur players. Mark, 14, is starting to beat Dad, which drives me crazy. I can't even beat Mom! For several hours after we get back to the cabin – despite Mom's best efforts – I'm inconsolable. Eventually this passes. Eventually, I'll accept the fact that Mark is a naturally gifted player and I'm not. I'll burst with pride when he becomes captain of the Cornell tennis team; even more when he and dad are ranked eighth in the nation in father-son doubles. Many years later – deep into middle age – I'll have mixed feelings when I get good enough to occasionally beat my big brother. Tennis has been a source of many highs for me. But I'll always be haunted by the lowest low – that melt-down I had as an 11 year old on that beautiful court in town overlooking the Hudson River. Because Mom never played another set with me.

It is 1973. I am 24 years old. Budding reporter. Pretty pleased with myself. I've just attended my first Fourth Lake community meeting. The issue at hand is whether to add an enclosed porch onto the community house, at a cost of $300. The elders go back and forth for an hour Then another hour. The debate is passionate, occasionally eloquent. Finally, everyone is exhausted. The question is called. The vote is 27-24 in favor of building the porch. After the meeting breaks up, I pay my compliments to one of the officers, a close friend of my parents.   "I've covered a lot of town meetings," I tell him. "This was the best debate I've ever heard." He puts his arm around me. "Kid," he says, "we always have great debates. They always go on for hours. And the vote is always 27-24."

It is 1998. I am 49 years old. The community's annual Potluck Dinner is winding down. I'm having a lovely chat with Doris, the community president. Back in the 1930s when they were teenagers, she and my mom were cub reporters on the staff of the Clarion, our community newspaper. They were friends and frenemies, sparring over story assignments and boys. (The editor was a handsome older teenager who went on to become one of the writers of the Superman comics). In the years since mom's death, Doris and I have grown close but we've never had anything beyond a perfunctory conversation about Mom. Tonight, she's had a few glasses of wine and is feeling mellow. "Let me tell you about your mom," Doris begins. I lean in, awaiting some sort of grace note or sweet memory. "She was such a stinker."

It is 2003. Stefanie and I are 54 years old. We are at the funeral for Michael Kamen, the incandescent light among our gang of Fourth Lake friends. His father Saul has the unimaginably sad task of eulogizing his son. Saul begins by quoting Michael: "Music has always been the language I speak best." Michael was a composer of both classical and rock music. A protean talent, he wrote the music for dozens of big budget movies, won three Grammys, two Golden Globes and an Emmy. He worked with Pink Floyd, Queen, Eric Clapton, Aerosmith, Tom Petty, Bon Jovi, David Bowie, Metallica, Bryan Adams and other rock and roll giants. He wore his celebrity lightly. He had a puckish wit. A gentle soul. A huge heart. It gave out on him at the age of 55, after a struggle with multiple sclerosis. How could he possibly be gone so young?

Saul was a dentist who pioneered techniques for treating special needs kids. His other passion was stand-up comedy. He knew a million jokes, most of them raunchy. What a hoot it was to be a young teenager listening to one of your friend's parents reel off a string of dirty jokes! All of them were of the Borscht Belt ilk. Period pieces. An acquired taste. Here's one:

> *Two women of a certain age are swimming in the ocean in Miami Beach. A big wave crashes over both of them. As they make their way out of the water, one reaches into her bosom, takes out a cigarette and lights it up.*
>
> *The other looks at her and says, "How did you do that?"*
>
> *The first woman says, "I'll tell you my secret. I wrap my cigarettes in a condom."*
>
> *That afternoon the second woman goes to her pharmacist. "I want to buy a condom."*
>
> *"We usually sell them in packs of three."*
>
> *"I only want one."*
>
> *What size?"*
>
> *[And now Saul puts on his thickest Eastern European accent]: "For a Camel."*

Saul also composed his own limericks:

There once was a young man from Sparta,
Who was a magnificent farter,
He could fart anything,
From God Save the King,
To Beethoven's Moonlight Sonata.

As I said, an acquired taste.

From her outpost in the community garage, where she ran the arts and crafts classes when we were little kids, Helen Kamen was a second mother to all of us. With her nurturing manner and ditzy humor, it was impossible not to adore her. But old age was not kind to Helen. She had health problems, then dementia. One day when Stef was out running, she found Helen in a confused state wandering in the middle of 9N, the two-lane state highway that bisects our community. Stefanie took Helen into her arms and told her she was taking her for a walk. When she brought her back to her family cabin, Helen grew angry. "Stefanie, I can't believe you of all people are turning me in!" She died a few months later.

Helen and Saul had four sons, all dear friends of ours. Michael and his older brother Paul are gone. Jon and Lenny are very much alive. So are a slew of Kamen grandchildren and now a first wave of great grandchildren. As long as there are Kamens, Fourth Lake will always be Fourth Lake.

It is 2024. We are finishing up a two-hour memorial service for Al Fertel, 87, the most joyful man ever to grace Fourth Lake. Al grew up in a family of bagel makers. He had an instinct for bringing out the best in everyone he met and a genius for helping everyone he met bring out the best in themselves. Dozens of us take turns telling stories about his exuberance, his generosity, his empathy, his love of children, his love of life, his love of mountain climbing, his love of campfires, his love for his family. Al's daughters Cindi and Judy bring the celebration to a close by reeling off, Letterman Style, their Top Ten List of Altruisms.

10) A fish that keeps its mouth shut never gets caught.

9) Guilt trips only work if you give permission to the person planning the trip.

8) You don't always have to tell your side of the story; time will do that for you.

7) Some things break your heart but correct your vision.

6) One thing about tables is that they always turn. They have before, and they will again.

5) Remember when you wanted everything you have now?

4) Be kind to schmucks. It will put a pep in your step.

3) I've had a lot of worries in my life, most of which never happened.

2) There is no greater bond in life than the one between the person who doesn't want their pickle and the person who wants an extra pickle.

1) The rules are that there are no rules!

Al was half a generation older than Stefanie and me. Now that he's gone, there aren't many Fourth Lakers left who are older than us and our childhood buddies. We're the elders! Crazy thought, after being treated as the kids for most of our adult lives. Still getting our minds around it.

In 2021, I was elected president of the Fourth Lake Community Association.[46] A big job back in the founders' era – when there was land to buy, by-laws to write, norms to establish. But it's mostly a care-taker position now. I basically have one assignment: Don't fix, ain't broke. It took me a while to figure this out. I spent the first few years of my tenure trying to nudge the community to address challenges we face as we keep producing more babies and needing more hous-es. We're bursting at the seams; the caps created decades ago by our forebears have begun to pinch. But change is scary. People worry that expansion could threaten "the us-ness of us," as one old timer put it. In time, when the unsparing arithmetic of generational family growth pinches even more, we'll make the needed changes. Folks aren't ready yet.

Meanwhile, I busy myself with potholes and lifeguards and inva-sive aquatic plants and the summer lecture series and the million little maintenance matters that come along. Happily, the actual work is done by our fourteen (!) standing committees and six (!!) ad hoc committees. I oversee, lightly. My most notable contribution is the newsletter I write (TWIFL, for This Week in Fourth Lake) that keeps everyone up to date on community doings and reminds us all how lucky we are to have each other, and this place. I specialize in glad tidings.

Even here in paradise, neighbors sometimes get into spats, where-upon I'm called on to be a rabbi or mediator or something of that ilk. Shortly after I was elected (needless to say, unopposed, this being a job no one actually wants) two members got into a terrible row over their dogs, one of which had bitten the other. I convened a pow-wow on my deck with the county dog catcher in attendance. Apologies

---

[46]   *One of the first things I did was hold a contest to see who could come up with a better name for the community. I was the lone judge. The two winners: Anatevka and Firth of Fourth. Not bad! Each winner received an ice cream cone. But the name it ain't a- chang-ing.*

were offered; pledges made. The dog fights have stopped. The raw feelings persist.

I console myself that I didn't let things deteriorate as badly as they once did, more than half a century ago, when a minor dispute between two neighbors escalated to the point that one erected a large "spite fence" on their common property line. The other neighbor thereupon circulated a petition that deplored the fence and demanded it be demolished. The first neighbor thereupon brought a civil suit, claiming slander and defamation. The case was heard by a county judge in nearby Glens Falls. He ruled for the plaintiff. Apparently unamused to have spent the court's time on the matter, he awarded damages of six cents.

That was Fourth Lake's most infamous spat, but my impression from stories I've heard is that things often got chippy back in the day. Perhaps this was because the stakes were higher, with the very existence of the community often at stake. Perhaps it was because there were constant disagreements about money, with roughly half the community unwilling to spend it on just about anything. (Thus all those 27-24 votes.)

Mercifully, we no longer have recurring budget fights. But we do have a low-grade tension around money. We're no longer a community mostly made up of middle-income school teachers and modest look-alike cabins. Now we are lawyers, doctors, professors, journalists, scientists, artists, engineers, economists, musicians, teachers, entrepreneurs. Most of us are comfortably upper middle class. A few of us are poor; a handful are extremely wealthy. In recent years several wealthy members have built humongous vacation homes that overlook the lake. Some Fourth Lakers, true to their fuck-capitalism DNA, are offended by the opulence. Others worry that the lights from the big houses intrude on the beloved rituals of our beach at night – campfires, star gazing, skinny dipping. Others say, hey, their property, their money, free country.[47] For their part, the wealthy owners – long-time and well-loved community members – have gone out of their way to address concerns about night lights. As for me, I listen closely to all parties and make it abundantly clear I agree with every one of them. I'm a born peacekeeper. Tensions simmer but do not singe.[48]

Two centuries ago America's most insightful observer from abroad, Alexis de Tocqueville, marveled at how a land that had been settled by rugged individualists was now bursting with social and civic associations. There was nothing like them in Europe, he wrote, and "nothing deserves more attention." He credited these bulwarks with providing the foundation for Americans' faith in democracy and their relentless pursuit of progress. But contemporary life has not been kind to de Tocqueville's America. We've become a nation of loners, not joiners. In his acclaimed 2000 book, *Bowling Alone,* sociologist Robert Putnam documented a long-term decline in voluntary associations. Since then the downward spiral has accelerated. In the past quarter century, America's churches have lost 40 million congregants; service clubs like Rotary, Kiwanis, Shriners and American Legion have withered; so have bowling leagues, sewing clubs and PTAs. Now we have Facebook, Instagram, TikTok and X.

Fourth Lake is a microscopic counter trend. On summer afternoons, two, three and sometimes four generations gather on our beach. We gossip. We swim. We boat. We sail. We read. We fish. We

---

[47]   *Our communitarian roots are marbled with libertarian tendencies. Most homeowners' associations have a long laundry list of rules about what folks can and can't do with their property. We have just two, designed to limit short-term rentals.*

[48]   *At the close of the summer of 2025, the second of my two terms having expired, I graduated to the role of elder statesman. Good gig!*

rest. We sleep. We play volleyball. We talk about politics and current events. We talk about what we're making for dinner tonight. We talk about restaurants, TV shows, movies, concerts. We keep an eye on the kids and grandkids – ours, everyone's.[49] We exchange medical advice. We do the crossword puzzle, Spelling Bee, Wordle. The afternoons are laid back, mundane, unremarkable, sublime. One thing we don't do is bury our heads in our cellphones. They're frowned upon (though not expressly forbidden). In a world that breeds loneliness, we foster connection. Here, friends are family. Community is a sanctuary. Becoming old does not mean becoming irrelevant.

Wendy Aronson baby-sat for me in the 1950s. She's six years older – an eternity then, the blink of an eye now. Funny how that works.

Unique among our contemporaries, Wendy has no biological family. She's an only child, her parents are long gone, she never had kids.

On her 50th birthday, shortly after she and her husband divorced, she sat cross-legged on the footbridge that leads across the creek to our lake and told herself: "This is my family now."

Wendy thinks of that as the moment she rescued the second half of her life. "As a kid I was secretly grateful for being an only child," she recalled. "I thought I was so lucky because I didn't have to share anything with anyone." But at that moment "I realized that wasn't going to work for me anymore. And if I didn't have a family of my own, I needed to create one."

---

[49]   *On especially delicious afternoons, when the kids are all playing nicely with each other, building elaborate sandcastles or digging glorious holes, Stef and I will smile over at our fellow grandparents and remark, "Wouldn't they made a lovely couple?"*

Wendy's father had been community president in the 1950s and 1960s. She spent her childhood summers marinated in all things Fourth Lake. Whip smart and fiercely independent, she became a gastroenterologist – this at a time when, she says, "the world wasn't quite ready for a woman who did rectals." Nevertheless, she built a thriving solo practice in Manhattan and married a fellow doctor. But he never "got" Fourth Lake. "He hated it here." So for decades Wendy limited her visits to periodic weekend check-ins to make sure her widowed mom was still able to take care of herself. Then came the divorce, and everything changed.

One hard truth about getting old is that your social networks shrink. This doesn't have to be a bad thing. Researchers have found that people who age successfully are selective in their choice of friends. They want deep connections rather than casual ones. It's great to have friends with whom you can share hobbies. But the real prize is something else: emotional support, an appreciation for life, a sense of meaning. Wendy nurtured many of those relationships in Fourth Lake in the second half of her life. And now, even though several of her closest friends have passed, she still draws enormous comfort just from being here.

"I dare you to find anyone who is less religious than me, but I have a deeply spiritual feeling about Fourth Lake. My eyes tear up at the start of every summer when my car turns onto Pine Tree Lane. It's incredible to return to a place where you know people's grandparents and their grandchildren. Where they knew your parents. Where they've known you your whole life. I have a place in the universe that belongs to me, that's a part of me. What a blessing."

Ann Schlitt's Fourth Lake bloodlines stretch back even farther than Wendy's. In 1915, her grandfather, Anton Buchbinder, was the first New York City school teacher to set foot here. Ann is a year older than

Stefanie and me. As kids we went on hayrides together. We've been friends ever since.

She got divorced when she was 70. Three years later she retired from her career as a television news producer. Now, she says, she spends her life "figuring out who I am when I'm not part of a couple and my identity isn't tied to my work."

One of her solutions speaks to the best of who we are. For the past two years she's been helping in a hundred ways, large and small, a fellow Fourth Laker who suffered a debilitating stroke. Many others in the community have also pitched in, but Ann's the one we're all ready to nominate for sainthood.

Like everyone our age, Ann has wistful memories of her younger self. "I miss my thicker, brown hair. I miss eyes that can see, ears that can hear. Being an older woman with gray hair means I'm less seen, even invisible. Sometimes that's ok, other times just sad."

For her, Fourth Lake has never been more important. "Growing old here is a gift. There are role models who've gone before who inspire us. There are contemporaries to commiserate with. There are young people to keep us young at heart. There's a strong support group in place. The bad? Only that I can't do all the things I used to do. Getting in and out of my kayak is a challenge now."

Ann's adaptation: "Try not to fight it. Accommodate your limitations, be they physical or mental. Make your expectations realistic. Be accepting."

Danny and April Levy are our community's most prolific grandparents. Their three sons and daughters-in-law have produced ten heirs in the past decade. They're also notable for another reason – one of just a handful of families who aren't part of Fourth Lake's blue tribe.

Our house is right across the street from theirs. We've known each other forever and grown close in old age. They're *mensches*.[50] When I asked what it's like to be part of a community whose prevailing political views are so different from theirs, April emailed me this account:

"I grew up in a family with a lengthy and prominent Communist pedigree. Everyone on my maternal grandfather's side was a Red (meant something different back then!) – even my rabbi grandfather. Two of his brothers were founders of *The Worker*. My mother was fired from her teaching job at Franklin K. Lane High School after being (justly, most likely) accused of preaching Communism in the classroom.

"I, on the other hand, felt ardent patriotism for the United States and all it stood for – and against. But I was not exactly a conservative back then. My political leanings went in various directions at various times. During the Vietnam War, I briefly joined SDS until the behavior of some of my fellow protestors on the March in Washington ended that connection.

"My voting record similarly points in various directions – and, as a result, I've often pulled the lever for third-party candidates. That's what I did the second time Obama ran after I'd voted FOR Obama the first time he ran. And the first time Trump was on the ballot, I voted for Evan McMullen – whoever he was! But in both 2020 and 2024 I pulled the lever enthusiastically for Trump, and, given the alternatives, I do not regret my choice.

"I don't feel alienated in Fourth Lake despite my minority leanings. I don't discuss politics much with most people here because there would be no point to it: the "Progressives" will not change my beliefs, and I know I won't change theirs. We coexist peacefully – something I wish would prevail in the

---

[50]   *Yiddish for great people.*

world beyond. I've felt bad on the rare occasions when political tensions have flared up here, but the divide is everywhere and far too often absolute and even vicious.

"Politics pale in comparison to what is far more important to me and, I think, most Fourth Lakers: friends, of course. Even more, family. Luzerne provides a family of families. In my strolls through the community, I'll often recall those who used to live among us and no longer do. This was so-and-so's house; so-and-so lived there. I hope, after we are gone, our grandchildren will be able to cherish the same memories."

April retired not long ago from her career as an educator. Danny, near retired, is a political science professor at SUNY-Albany; his specialty is Latin American politics. Over the years, his community lectures and frequent trips abroad have led some here to wonder if he had a side job with the CIA. (Sound familiar?) "Well, here's your belated scoop," Danny told me. "Yes, but in no clandestine way that would excite my grandkids." He periodically provides the agency with his analysis of political dynamics in that part of the globe.

Like April, Danny said that politics have barely intruded on his Fourth Lake life. "I did have a minor youth rebellion against whatever sympathy our parents' generation retained for Communism and the USSR. References to 'your conservative son' occasionally insulted my mother. But April and I were close with many of my parents' friends, and I learned that 'Communism' had been largely a moral response to closely witnessed suffering."

To April's paeans to the joys of grandparenting in Fourth lake, Danny added a poignant coda. "The most natural grandparent imaginable, my father, was denied any grandparenting opportunity [Morris Levy died at 67]. Now, as we contemplate our own departures, nothing soothes like the expanding lives of his great grandchildren."

CHAPTER FOURTEEN

"GRADUALLY, THEN SUDDENLY"

Fall, 2025

What that Hemingway character said about going bankrupt also applies to growing old. Maybe not for everyone, but absolutely for me. Right up until I turned 70, I barely gave old age a thought. It was something that happened to other folks, not to me. Aside from my knees, I was still a kid.

That was then. Now I'm old and I know it. I suppose it's a good thing that I've finally surrendered to reality. But it's no fun.

The tipping point has been my knees, my goddamn knees. They used to be a mere nuisance. Now, I think about them the moment I climb out of bed. Whenever I walk. Whenever I sit. Whenever I stand. Whenever I'm on a flight of stairs. Up is a grind, down a misery. On good days I wince. On bad days, I descend sideways.

On any hierarchy of late-in-life insults to the body, creaky knees rank near the bottom. I know that. But they've mounted an assault on my self-image. I used to be graceful, quick, supple, light on my feet. I used to skip downstairs. I miss that guy.

It's unbecoming that this bothers me so much. I have other signs of aging that ought to freak me out but somehow don't. For example, I can't remember a goddamn thing. And no, I'm not just talking about those senior moments we all have. I'm talking about this: I'll be writing something, then I'll get interrupted for some reason and I'll put my pen down. Then, maybe 30 seconds or a minute later, I'm ready to resume but I have no fucking idea where my pen went. I have the memory of a flea.[51]

Happily, there's a solution for that: Buy more pens! And more reading glasses. And more screwdrivers. And more flashlights. And so on. As for all the other stuff I can't remember – names, dates, facts, what I had for dinner last night, where I left my keys, etc.– I try to see the glass half full.[52] Like every other human who's ever lived, I've been losing millions of brains cells every year since puberty. Grateful to have a handful left.

Why can't I bring that same equanimity to my gait? I fear it comes down to vanity. Nobody can see my forgetfulness. Everyone can see my gait.

If you're a sports fan of my vintage, you'll remember Earl the Pearl Monroe, maybe the most acrobatic basketball player ever to step onto a court. He juked and jived and improvised. "I had no idea

----

[51] *The other night in bed, I couldn't come up with the second verse of "Row, Row, Row Your Boat." Of all the ridiculous things! Took me maybe 30 seconds before a light bulb finally flickered. Aha! "Life is but a dream!" Yup, feels that way.*

[52] *As W.C. Fields put it, "I have a terrible memory for names, but I seldom recall a face." Q: Do my memory deficits make me an unreliable narrator of my own memoir? I worry about that. Many stories in this book are memories of memories. I no longer remember the events themselves; I only remember the stories I've told about them over the years. I'm a reporter – I try hard to get things right. But we all know what happens to stories as they get told and retold. So, caveat emptor.*

where he was going because he had no idea where he was going," said Walt Frazier, the Knicks guard who played against him and later with him. "Not even God could cover Earl the Pearl."

A few months ago, Monroe, 80, made a rare public appearance at a ceremony honoring one of his old Knicks teammates. He arrived in a wheelchair. Thirteen years in the NBA had been the prelude to a lifetime of surgeries.

After the event was over Monroe told reporters that appearing in front of television cameras alongside basketball's aristocracy "was traumatic for me – the world seeing me like that. I'm a shell of myself at this point. I'm very depressed about it. I don't like to do things, going here and going there, because I'm pretty vain. I don't want people to remember me as a cripple after you've seen me as I was." Feel your pain, brother.

⁓

So what now? I have to adapt. Understood. But how?

Let's start by taking stock. In the old age sweepstakes, where do Stefanie and I stand? Stefanie is happy to be standing at all. Earlier this year she spent a few weeks flat on her back, nursing the foot she broke when she knocked a frozen chicken she never saw out of the freezer onto the base of her middle toe. This was her third vision-related bone break in the past two years. In our son's kitchen, she tripped and broke two ribs. Back in our kitchen, she toppled a blender and cracked her pinkie toe.

Her world continues to shrink, even by the standards of periscope vision. She now uses a white cane when she's in a grocery store or any other crowded indoor space. She likes the way it announces: Beware: You can see me; I can't see you. Outdoors, she finds the cane less useful. It can save her from potholes and curbs, but not from overhanging branches and distracted drivers.[53] There, she prefers the security of hiking sticks. When something goes awry, she has a better shot at staying upright.

Aside from Stef's eyes, we're heathy. But – memo to kids and grandkids – when you get to be our age, "healthy" is a moving target. Even if you're lucky like us and dodge the dreaded age-related diseases that lay in wait – cancer, heart attacks, diabetes, strokes, dementia – your body parts will start wearing out. And you'll have to keep hauling yourself into the shop for repairs.

Along with her four eye specialists, Stef has ten other doctors she sees periodically. My medical Rolodex isn't that big yet but it's getting there. What do we do with ourselves now that we're old? Glad you asked! We go to the doctor! What do we talk about with our friends? Glad you asked!! We talk about our operations, procedures, symptoms, conditions, medications, appointments, recoveries, insurance policies, organs, body parts. Much of the time we're laughing at ourselves, playing can-you-top-this? So that can be kinda fun. Still, a strange way to live. Maybe I'm misremembering, but I could swear that when we were young, whole years went by without either of us ever going to a doc. Now it feels like we shoehorn our lives in between our doc visits, not the other way around.

Clams live for hundreds of years. I don't envy them. Salamanders live shorter lives but stay spry till the very end. I do envy that.

I don't like the way old age comes on like some cosmic practical joke, with me as its straight man. It's not just that my body and mind

---

[53] *Our great friend David Tatel, a retired U.S. Appeals Court Judge, is Stefanie's most trusted tour guide into the land of the blind. David lost all his vision when he was in his twenties. He spent most of his life using a cane and for years encouraged Stef to get one. When she finally did, she commiserated with him over dinner one night. "You can still get whacked in the face," she said. "Tell me about it!" David agreed. "They can be a total disaster!" A few years ago he got a guide dog, which he wrote about in loving detail in his marvelous memoir, Vision. (David, BTW, is the judge whose lap took the brunt of that toppled wine glass at that memorable dinner party with Teddy Kennedy.)*

keep sliding backward. It's that technology keeps lurching forward, leaving me dazed, confused, infantilized.

Is there such a thing as a tech savvy 77-year-old? I'd like to meet you. When I get hung up in password protection purgatory, can you extradite me? Can you rid me of the non-stop texts hawking medical devices, burial insurance, Medicare plans? Can you protect me from subscription scams and junk fees? Can you rescue me when my TV remotes stop talking to each other? When my cellphone no longer syncs with my tablet? When my doctor emails a message in an app I can't open? Can you tell me whether to enable cookies or disable them? Stef and I would be most appreciative; our kids even more so. Nowadays, when they visit, the first order of business is for them to work through everything we've added to their IT to-do list since their previous visit.

Frank Bruni says that codgers and technology go together like sardines and peanut butter. But for me this isn't just an old age problem. I've been a technophobe most of my life.[54] And Stef, you'll recall, has always been a Luddite. With her vision slipping away, she relented a year ago and taught herself to send and receive texts by voice command. We now share our home with Siri and Alexa. They can be good helpers, but this too can go off the rails. On days when they deliver different weather forecasts – which for some reason happens a lot when we're up in Fourth Lake – Stefanie will get rather cross. I don't know about your Siris and Alexas, but ours know all about the f-word.

---

[54]   *You know those classic anxiety dreams – you never studied for the big test; you neglected to get dressed before going to work, etcetera? In my old age, all of my anxiety dreams revolve around technology. A typical plot: I've written up a big story on deadline, but I can't get my computer to transmit it. When I was in Africa, I worried all the time about computer glitches. But I never had these dreams back then. Why am I having them now? Ideas, anyone? And while I'm at it, does anybody know how I can get my Superman dreams back?*

How did this happen?? Wasn't it just yesterday that we got by without arguing with our gadgets? When I was winning tennis tournaments? Rebuilding a house? Skipping down stairs?

Those days are gone and ain't coming back. Good grief, get over it. Stop bitching. Start adapting!

But how?

For Stef and me, it starts with accepting the fact that the decisions we need to make from here on out are different from the ones we faced when we were younger. Then, life was all about seizing opportunity. Now, it's mostly about managing decline. If someone had told our younger selves that our number one job in old age would simply be to stay healthy, I suspect we'd have both rolled our eyes and said get us the Hell out of here. But here we are.

Staying healthy is about more than doctors, meds, diets and exercise. It's figuring out how to hang on to your identity when there are no longer any work emails in the inbox; when you can't make jewelry; when the world seems capable of getting along just fine without you.

Today's decisions may not be as exciting as yesterday's but are every bit as challenging. How do we make sure we'll still be able to care for each other, come what may? Should we install ramps? Sell the Bethesda house? Buy a condo? Check out independent living? With levels?

"Nothing is more delusional about getting older than thinking that you're going to have time to 'take it easy.'" writes Sari Botton, 60, author, editor and publisher of Oldster Magazine. "Aging well is hard work, demanding nonstop vigilance, awareness and fearlessness, plus you have to deal with a really weird dynamic – always being good to your body while it's intent on betraying you."

New Age writer and anthropologist Carlos Castaneda put it this way: "To be young and vital is nothing. To be old and vital is sorcery."

Everyone knows the expression: "Age is just a number." For most of my male friends, there's one number in particular that's top of mind – the age their father was when he died. It means different things to different guys. A floor, a ceiling, a target, a warning, a reminder. But it's always there.

My dad died at 83. As I close in on his number, I think about him more and more. How did he live? What made him tick? What did he leave behind? How have I lived? What will I leave behind?

As a young boy growing up in a middle-class Jewish neighborhood in Brooklyn, his grand ambition was to see the world, experience the world, conquer the world. When he graduated from college at age 19, he changed his last name from Schwartzberg to Taylor, a nod to his paternal grandfather, who had been a tailor in the old country.[55] Dad wanted to be a diplomat and he knew that the State Department back then wasn't a hospitable place for Jews. As soon as he turned 21, he took the written entrance exam and passed with flying colors. But he failed the oral exam, probably because he was young and callow. And perhaps because the examiners could spot the Schwartzberg hiding behind the Taylor. In his later years, he made gentle fun of his younger self: "With invincible innocence, I asked of life only two little baubles: power and wisdom…I wanted to be in the battle at the head of the troops, as well as above it looking on."

---

[55]   *Might my life have been different had I lived it as Paul Schwartzberg? No idea. But I do have a fond and funny memory of one moment when my religious identity had an impact on my professional life. It came on the day I interviewed for a job at the Washington Post. Late in the afternoon, after meetings with a string of mid-level and senior editors, I was ushered into Ben Bradlee's office. He had my clips and resume on his desk. We shook hands. He looked me in the eye. "Tell me," he began in his famously gravelly voice, "what are WASPs like us doing in a business like this?" "Well actually I'm Jewish," I replied, "evidently assimilated." Ben smiled. "Evidently," he said, then peppered the rest of the interview with Yiddish expressions. And that, as someone once said in the movies, was the start of a beautiful friendship.*

Hopes thwarted, dad spent his twenties working with his father in the garment industry. A rich learning experience, he'd later write, but not what he wanted from life. He turned to politics and became executive director of the Manhattan branch of the Liberal Party. When he was in his mid-30s, he used his political and labor union connections to land that long-sought job in the Foreign Service. By then he'd married mom – a beautiful, high-spirited young woman from the neighborhood and his kid sister's good friend –and Mark and I had arrived.

Our family spent three years in Japan and another 18 months in Vietnam. Then dad quit abruptly. My brother and I grew up believing he had become frustrated with the State Department bureaucracy. Decades later - after mom's death – I learned that it was mom's bout with depression that led us back to the States.

Dad reentered the world of politics as Manhattan director of the Americans for Democratic Action, a liberal, anti-communist political interest group founded by Eleanor Roosevelt. In 1960 he became an ardent early supporter of John F. Kennedy, writing policy papers and offering advice on how to win over New York City's liberal leaders, most of whom preferred Adlai Stevenson or Hubert Humphrey for the Democratic presidential nomination. After Kennedy won the presidency, Dad lobbied for – but never got – a policy job in the new administration. This was surely the biggest disappointment of his professional life, but he never betrayed a hint of grievance to my brother and me. Privately, in his voluminous unpublished papers, he concluded that he was too cerebral and guileless for a life in politics. I think he was right about that.

He spent the remaining two decades of his career as executive director of the US Japan Trade Council, a Washington DC-based lobbying group. A good job, but not his passion. His passion was his writing. He would wake up every morning at dawn and spend a few hours before heading off to work writing essays, articles, book reviews, op-ed columns and letters-to-the-editor. His favorite topics were civil rights, race, gender, religion, ethics, foreign policy and whatever popped up in the morning headlines. He also produced four book-length manuscripts – a non-believer's critique of God; a dissertation on liberty and equality; a reflection on the meaning of freedom, and a personal memoir. Almost everything he wrote went unpublished, a fate he accepted with puzzlement and grace as he kept on writing.

When I became a newspaper reporter and achieved some success, Dad urged me to set my sights on becoming the columnist he wished he had been. But we weren't wired the same way. I didn't have the temperament or skills to get up on a soap box each day and tell people how they should be living their lives and politicians how they should be running their countries. My calling was to inform, not to persuade. I just wanted to get the facts right and the story straight, so people could figure for themselves how best to act on them. When I left journalism to become a public interest advocate, it wasn't to promote an ideological or policy agenda. It was to create a public square in which the best information could get to the greatest number of people in the most user-friendly way at the most important time, right before an election. Dad was disappointed by my career move – more, I suspect, than he let on to me. But we had some good talks about our different personalities and aspirations. We came to understand each other well, I think. I've spent my life awed by his intellect and grateful to have inherited his values. I wish he had more emotional intelligence, especially given what happened to Mom. He felt the same way about himself and took that regret to his grave.

A few months before Dad died, he asked me to hit some tennis balls with him. We hadn't played in quite a while. He was having trouble with his eyes, and his game had deteriorated. He needed to decide whether to sign up for another season of indoor winter doubles with a group of men he'd been playing with for decades. We hit for about a half hour before he called the session off. The next day he wrote a lovely note to his buddies thanking them for all the great years and telling them he didn't want to drag down the level of the game. It was time for him to give up tennis.

In their prime, Dad and Mark were ranked eighth in the country.

That was the beginning of the end. Over the next several months, he went into a physical and cognitive free fall. There was no precipitating event. The doctors surmised that he'd had a series of mini strokes, each difficult to detect. He spent most of his final month in a rehab facility – weak, bed-bound, incontinent and confused, telling stories that mixed up events that had happened that morning with events that had happened fifty years before. He did manage to convey that he wanted out of that facility. The doctors felt he wasn't ready, but my step-mother and I chose to honor his wishes. We brought Dad back to their apartment. He died the following week, of sepsis, after a short stay in the hospital. It was on Christmas Day. Maybe God was making a point.

It's been two years since my retina surgery and a year since follow-up cataract surgery. I can manage everyday life fine. But even with new glasses that have prisms in the lenses, it still takes me too long to figure out how fast a tennis ball is coming at me. I'm getting cortisone shots and lubricating gels injected into my knees a few times a year. This gives me some okay knee days to go along with all the lousy knee days. But even on good days, those knees can no longer get me around a tennis court.

A few months ago I sent my tennis buddies an email to let them know I'll be retiring from our winter doubles group. Don't want to bring down the level of play. I'll still see them socially, but I've said goodbye to a loyal friend. The game of tennis.

Even so, I've come around to a more balanced view of aging. This, too, happened gradually then suddenly. Actually, it happened in the course of writing this memoir. Like many writers, I write to figure out what I think. Now, when I re-read the opening chapter I wrote a few years ago, I find myself thinking, hmm, too strong?

I still agree with Philip Roth: "Old age is not a battle. Old age is a massacre." Haven't changed my mind about that. But there are compensations that I'm finally getting my mind around. Aging brings a heightened appreciation for life's blessings. More emotional resilience. More space to not sweat the small stuff. More wisdom about how to nurture relationships. A deeper understanding of what you were meant to do with your brief time on this earth. And if you're lucky like me, a sense of fulfillment about the journey you've taken.

Stefanie has also made peace with old age. But she still has her Plan B. "I've always lived life on my own terms. And I'm going to keep living that way. If I ever get to the point when I can't, I want to be like the athlete who knows when it's time to retire. If I'm lucky, I'll never get to that point. So far, so good."

Have the two of us found the secrets to aging well? Some, perhaps. But here's one riddle I'm still stuck on: Should I be guided by the ancient wisdom of Taoism, which instructs the elderly that, having done our worldly work, we should take a step back and dwell in contentment and serenity. This strikes me as the soul of wisdom. But the modern guru I most admire, Marc Freedman,[56] preaches the opposite: the deepest joy in old age comes from living a purpose-driven life right up until you draw your last breath. This too strikes me as the soul of wisdom.

For now, I've got one leg striding down each path, achy knees and all. Will I solve this riddle by the time I'm 80? 90? 100? We'll see.

---

[56] *Marc is the founder of Encore (now called CoGenerate), a non-profit group that helps older adults find meaning in the second half of their lives by working on projects that improve the lives of children and young adults.*

CHAPTER FIFTEEN

LOVE, GRANDPA

Dear Sabine, Clementine, Skye, Terra and Zoey,

When Jeremy was five years old, I took him to see *The Empire Strikes Back*. This was his first trip to a movie theater, and boy was he psyched! Me too. I'd been blown away by the first *Star Wars* movie and couldn't wait to take my little boy to the sequel.

Once the movie began, I could barely contain myself. Fearing that Jeremy might have trouble making sense of all the strange-looking creatures on the big screen, I would blurt out at key moments: "He's a good guy!" "He's a bad guy!"

After a few rounds of this, Jeremy tugged at my sleeve. "Daddy, shush!" he said. "I *know* who the good guys and bad guys are!"

I think this was probably my best ever lesson in parenting. Our job is to make sure our kids know right from wrong, but Jeremy taught me to tread lightly, teach by example, show don't tell.

Here I am now, half a lifetime later, thrilled to be watching each of you grow up. And once again, I'm having trouble controlling myself. So apologies in advance for what I'm about to do – which is ignore the advice I got long ago from your dad and uncle. As I bring this memoir to a close, I'm feeling an irresistible urge to pass along some grandfatherly wisdom. Old age has its privileges. Bear with me.

If you're in the market for an all-purpose guide for how to live your lives, there's nothing better than the Golden Rule. Do unto others as you would have others do unto you. My mom's favorite. Mine too. Here's more:

Be kind, be empathetic, be generous, be honest, work hard, be persistent, be curious, be an explorer. Follow your dreams. Try to leave the world better than you found it.

Find something you love to do, then keep doing it. When you get knocked down (and you will), pick yourself up. Learn from your failures. You'll do better next time.

The most important friend you can make is yourself. Make demands. Set high standards. But cut yourself some slack too. Don't expect to be perfect. Nobody is.

Nurture your friendships. Cherish your family. Find someone new to love. Create a family of your own. There's no greater joy.

Each of you is a miracle. Each of you represents something unique, something that never existed before. The same is true for every human being who's ever lived.

What are we all doing here? What's the purpose of our lives? Is there a God above who created all of us and keeps tabs on all of us?

My dad spent his whole life wrestling with those questions. His answer was that there is no God. It's up to each one of us to choose right over wrong, good over evil. It's up to each of us to keep score.

My mom's answer was that God is the love that lives within us.

I think they're both right.

My dad thought the best way to find the truth – about God and everything else – is to use your mind. My mom thought the best way to find the truth is to follow your heart.

I think they're both right about that too! Sometimes an idea and its opposite are both true. It took me a long time to figure that out. Maybe you'll make a similar discovery as you get older.

One thing you've already learned from this memoir is that getting old brings its share of aches, pains, sorrows and woes. Even for people like grandma and me, who've led such fortunate lives. I fear there's no escaping that.

But it also brings joys beyond measure. The best part of our remaining years will be spent watching our children launch their children – you, the miraculous you – into adulthood.

It's a big world. It wants to be your friend. Embrace it. Get out where love, and luck, can find you. Grandma and I will be cheering for you like crazy at every step of the way. Even after we're gone, we'll be with you always.

AFTERWORD

Writers need swagger. To get cranked up each morning, we need to feel, right down to the tips of our typing fingers, that we've got a helluva story to tell. This is doubly true for a memoir writer, since our great story is ourself.

When I told Stefanie I was thinking of writing this memoir, you'll recall that she said she doubted anyone – other than family – would read it. I replied that our difficulties in old age are interesting and relatable. They'll make a good story! Warily, she let me proceed.

That conversation was six years ago. Since then I've set aside the manuscript more times than I can count as I, too, struggled with doubt. Look at all the stuff I never did! Never got famous; never rose to the top of a profession; never had to overcome a tormented childhood, an addiction, a crisis of faith, a failed marriage, a tabloid scandal. My life has been happy, loving, lucky, stable, sane. Not much of a plot.

Nevertheless, each time I lost my swagger, I had no trouble finding where I'd put it. The doubts persisted, but I'd hooked one reader and hooked him hard. Me. I kept hoping to discover the secret to aging well. So I kept coming back to the manuscript.

Alas, no epiphanies ever popped. No tidy endings either. You grow old, you make peace with your losses, you celebrate everything you still have, you realize you're not as smart as you thought you were. You're frustrated, humbled, grateful. The search for meaning is the meaning. The journey is the destination. Life goes on.

I'm still not sure if this story works for others, but I'm certain that writing it has been good for me. It has given me a sense of purpose – at this stage of the game, a precious gift. Now that I'm done, I'll need to find something new. Stefanie and I are kicking around a few ideas.

Stefanie's Afterword

Paul has written a lot of cool things about me. Take them with a grain of salt. He's trying to make up for the boulders!

Kidding aside, I should clarify one thing about our 57 years together. He's not the only one who's gotten pretty much everything he wants from the relationship. So have I.

Even though I've had my misgivings about his book, I let him publish it for two reasons. It's obviously important to him. And it's become clear to me how important that conversations about growing old are to just about everyone our age.

I can be at a drug store, doctor's office or grocery and wind up trading stories with total strangers about our adventures caring for elderly parents.

Now that I'm getting along in years myself, I have lots of conversations with my friends about our own next adventures, with all the moving targets and health unknowns. Will we be any better than our parents at old age?

Last summer at a dinner in Fourth Lake, my brother Lee asked all of us around the table whether our lives had measured up to our expectations. I said I've never spent much time dreaming about what might be. I've taken life as it comes. It's almost always come easily. Lately, some bumps.

What I didn't say then were the first words that came to mind. "It's been a great ride."

Or the ones I'll add now: Feels like there are still some good miles left.

ACKNOWLEDGEMENTS

Dozens of friends and relatives read drafts of this book as it was being written. I reached out knowing I was putting them in a bit of a bind. It's hard to critique a manuscript written by someone you care about; harder still if it's a memoir. But they handled my queries with grace. I'm grateful for their fact checks, criticisms, suggestions, encouragements, sharp pencils. And their friendship and love. Each of them made the book better, in ways large and small. Thanks everyone.

A few public acknowledgements are in order:

My friend and agent, Peter Bernstein, tried valiantly to find a traditional publisher. His only reward was a collection of lovely rejection notes. After a while, it dawned on both of us: What I'm selling, they ain't buying. Thanks for trying, Peter.

So I moved along to Plan B – self-publishing. Thanks to the internet and social media, this method of selling books is a bona fide business. But learning the ropes is intimidating, especially for an older gent who has his share of tech phobias. Rich Carnahan, founder of the aptly-named Publish Pros, LLC, guided me with patience, skill, seasoned judgment and a gentle hand. Thank you, Rich.

Speaking of pros, Barbara Beck roared out of retirement to serve as this book's publicist. Barbara has been a great pal for half a century and, with her husband Larry, is a charter member of our vaunted New Year's Eve DIY Dinner Party Gang. She spent the first half of her career as a journalist and the second half running a small firm that helped non-profits promote their good works. Her smarts and enthusiasms are legendary. Her only condition for taking on this assignment was that she not be paid. Yo, girl – you drive a hard bargain. Thanks.

Now for a shout-out to my favorite tribe – the reporters who go out every day in search of the truth. You are my heroes. And America's too, even though our fellow citizens are rarely inclined to show the love. Your work is indispensable to my thinking and writing. It's indispensable to our democracy. Thanks, one and all. Keep hacking away.

The most important acknowledgement goes to my best friend, my best reader, my best editor, my best critic and my best character.

Stefanie is a very private person. In her heart of hearts, she'd rather I hadn't written this book. But she knew this was a story I wanted to tell. Needed to tell. So she gave me her blessing.

I'm relieved to report that she's okay with the book, save for one lingering criticism. She thinks I've portrayed her in colors too vivid.

I think I've gotten her just right.

We've agreed to disagree about that.

Thank you, my love.

www.ingramcontent.com/pod-product-compliance
Lightning Source LLC
Chambersburg PA
CBHW051515150726
47997CB00001B/260